WALKING IN THE LOWTHER HILLS

LOWTHER and OTHER HILLS: OVERVIEW

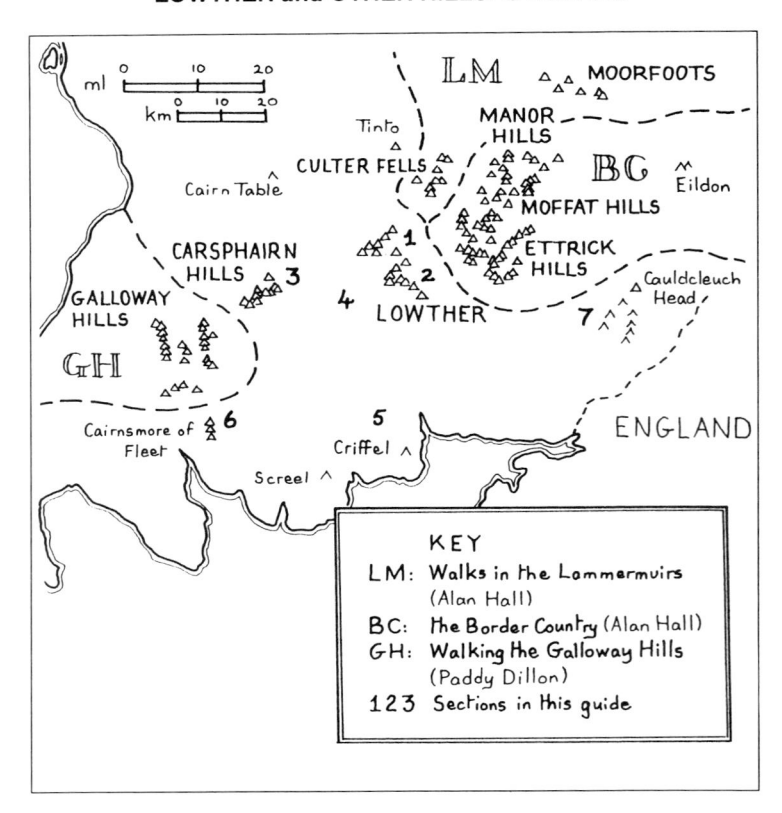

KEY
- LM: Walks in the Lammermuirs (Alan Hall)
- BC: the Border Country (Alan Hall)
- GH: Walking the Galloway Hills (Paddy Dillon)
- 1 2 3 Sections in this guide

WALKING IN THE LOWTHER HILLS
also
Carsphairn, Hills of the Solway Coast
Tinto and Cauldcleuch Head

by
Ronald Turnbull

CICERONE PRESS
MILNTHORPE, CUMBRIA

© R. Turnbull 1999
ISBN 1 85284 275 X
A catalogue record for this book is available from the British Library

> **Advice to Readers**
>
> Readers are advised that whilst every effort is taken by the author to ensure the accuracy of this guidebook, changes can occur which may affect the contents. It is advisable to check locally on transport, accommodation, shops etc but even rights-of-way can be altered.
>
> The publisher would welcome notes of any such changes

Front cover: Toll Cottage, Cleuch (Walks 2 & 3)

CONTENTS

Introduction 7
    Walking conditions 8
    Maps 8
    Access 9
    How to Use this Guide 10
    Geology 12
    The Covenanters 13

1: **NORTHERN LOWTHERS** 15
* 1:1 Lowther Hill, Green Lowther and the Mines 16
  1:2 Elvan Water: Louise to Lowther 19
* 1:3 Mennock Pass 22
** 1:4 Around the Enterkin 26
  1:5 Sanquhar to Stood Hill 30
  1:6 Steygail Scramble 34
** 1:7 Enterkin and Well Passes 35

2: **SOUTHERN LOWTHERS** 38
  2:1 Gana Hill, Ballencleuch Law from Daer 39
  2:2 Comb Law 42
* 2:3 Lavern Burn and Toll Cottage Cleuch 44
** 2:4 Well Hill and Pass, Penbane, Black Hill 47
* 2:5 Glenimp 50
  2:6 Glengap and Wedder Law 53
** 2:7 Kettleton and Cample 54
* 2:8 Queensberry from Mitchellslacks 58
  2:9 Queensberry from the East 63

3: **NITHSDALE** 66
* 3.1 Tynron Doon 67
  3.2 Drumlanrig and the Nith 68
* 3.3 Drumlanrig Woodland Walks 71
  3.4 Morton Castle and Lochs 72
** 3.5 Crichope Linn 73
  3.6 Glenkiln Sculptures and Bennan 74

4: **CARSPHAIRN HILLS** 78
* 4.1 Cairnsmore from Carsphairn 81
* 4.2 Windy Standard and Cairnsmore 83

5

THE LOWTHER HILLS

	4.3	Ewe Hill 87
**	4.4	Blackcraig, Blacklorg from Afton 91
	4.5	Euchan Top with Blacklorg Hill 94
	4.6	Euchan Bottom: Cloud Hill and Euchan Water 96
*	4.7	Glenwhargen Crag and Cairnkinna 100
		Galloway Hills from the Glenkens 102

5:	SOLWAY COAST 104	
**	5.1	Criffel from New Abbey 104
*	5.2	Waterloo Monument 107
	5.3	Boreland Hill and Criffel 110
	5.4	Criffel from Ardwall 112
	5.5	Mabie Forest and Marthrown Hill 113
	5.6	Mabie Forest Walks 115
**	5.7	Sandyhills Coast 117
**	5.8	Screel and Bengairn 122
*	5.9	Balcary Point 124

6:	CAIRNSMORE OF FLEET 129	
**	6.1	Cairnsmore of Fleet from Cairnsmore 130
*	6.2	Cairnsmore and the Clints 133
*	6.3	Cairnsmore from Talnotry 137
	6.4	Talnotry Trail 140
	6.5	Cairnsmore of Dee, Fell of Fleet 142
	6.6	Whithorn Coast and St Ninian's Cave 145

7:	OUTLYING HILLS 148	
*	7.1	Cairn Table and the Old Sanquhar Road 148
*	7.2	Tinto Hill 152
	7.3	Tinto and Lochlyock 155
	7.4	Cauldcleuch Head 157
	7.5	Circuit of Twislehope Hope 159
*	7.6	Whita Hill, Langholm 161
*	7.7	Annan Banks to Burnswark 165
*	7.8	Hoddom Castle Short Trails and Annan Banks to Hoddom 168

APPENDIXES 170
A: Longer outings 170
B: Other sports 172
C: Transport, accommodation, information 174

INTRODUCTION

Drive off the top end of the M6 on your way to the Highlands and you pass a place called Beattock Summit. On either hand lie some rather flat, rather low hills. Green forest embellishes their lower slopes, yellow grass their gentle summits.

This is a trick, perpetrated in the interest of road safety. You already terrified your passengers driving up the Lune Valley while looking over your shoulder at the Howgills. They're only just recovering, and it wouldn't do to terrify them again just 50 miles up the road. So the interesting hills are carefully concealed behind yellow grass and gentle slopes.

So take the next pass west, the A702 through Dalveen, and see something rather reminiscent of those Howgills. Steep grass rises on either side, neatly cut by stream cleuchs. Here and there a rock peeps through the velvety green covering: these hills have bones to them. Forgotten drove roads slant up the valley side. West again is the Mennock Pass, where you see the same thing done in heather mixture.

So while these hills offer grassy ridgewalking, they also offer a little bit more in the exploration of the stream hollows, the holes in the hill where the wild goats hang out and where you may find yourself involved with a small waterfall and a couple of feet of rock-climbing. I like to combine these two sorts of ground into a day or half-day's walking.

Along the Galloway coast are hills of a different sort: smaller, but fiercer. These granite lumps look across the Solway to the Lake District, and have a touch of Lakeland wildness themselves, with boulders everywhere, little bits of black bog and heather. They culminate in Cairnsmore of Fleet: a high-altitude, high-rainfall small wilderness of international importance. Its peat bog, granite slab and black heather combine to make one of Britain's top small mountains.

The Galloway Highlands are not part of the territory of this guide. The Merrick and Rhinns of Kells are covered in the publisher's companion volume *Walking the Galloway Hills* by Paddy Dillon. Hills to the east of the M74 (soon to be M6) motorway are in Alan

THE LOWTHER HILLS

Hall's two books *Walks in the Lammermuir Hills* and *The Border Country*. However, two fine two-thousanders managed to slip through the net, and so Tinto Hill in Lanarkshire and Cauldcleuch Head in Roxburghshire are scooped into this, the best of the rest of the Southern Uplands.

This is a book of hills, not mountains: but hills with rather more to them than grass, sheep and solitude. I hope you will enjoy, as I have done, getting into the hidden stream valleys, discovering the odd small crag, and wandering in mist, rain or cool sunlight over these wide and empty lands.

WALKING CONDITIONS
These grassy hills and ridges offer easy walking, even though there are no paths. The main problem arises when the mist comes down. Route-finding is then quite difficult on the featureless slopes. Basic map-and-compass work is essential. A map that marks the fences, such as Harveys, is also a great help.

Those fences provide one of the lesser problems. Some of them are electric. The routes in this book should take you to gates in fences. However, if you are confronted with an electric fence, there are various ways to proceed. You can put one hand on a fence-post and simply hop over - this is easier than you'd think. A shepherd will go to the midpoint between two of the widely-spaced posts and push down the wire with his stick until he can step over it. You can also press down the fence with a rubber-soled boot to let your companions over.

Although the hills are not high, they are high enough to offer unpleasant weather from time to time. Waterproof clothing and a spare warm layer will usually be carried, as in any other hill country. Winter conditions deserve respect: there have been deaths by avalanche in the Southern Uplands.

Several of the walks cross steep grassy slopes. These can be alarming in unsuitable shoes. Hill footwear has deep-cut soles of rubber.

MAPS
The maps in this book are impressionistic rather than accurate. For instance, the scratchy marks indicating the edge of high ground do

not correspond to any actual contour line - the highest point of Walk 5:8 (Screel Hill) is lower than the car park of Walk 1:1 (Wanlockhead). The maps at the beginnings of sections can be used to link the walks together into longer ones.

For finding the way on the ground, there are the useful Landranger (pink cover) maps of the Ordnance Survey. Sheets 77 and 78 cover the main part of the book. Two other maps are also available:

Harveys *Lowther Hills* covers sections 1 and 2. This map is smaller, cheaper and more waterproof than the Landranger. It marks field boundaries (fences or walls) where these are on the open hill, and also forest rides. While Landranger is adequate, this map is better.

OS Outdoor Leisure 32 (Galloway) covers section 6, and Cairnsmore of Carsphairn (Walk 4:1), as well as the Galloway Hills. It has good contour detail, and again marks fences and walls. However, it is very large and cumbersome, is not waterproof, and does not mark the forest rides.

ACCESS

Only one route in this book is on definite rights-of-way: Walk 1:7 (Enterkin and Well Passes). Many of the routes are on asserted rights-of-way, but most rely on the traditional tolerance by Scottish landowners of walkers on open uplands. Walkers will help preserve this tolerance by respecting legitimate land uses:

Lambing Time

Lambing on the uplands is from mid-March to the end of May. When passing sheep, keep dogs on leads and walk round the edges of fields. Fields with very young lambs are best avoided altogether, as disturbance may separate them from their mothers.

Sheep lying on their backs or with heads stuck in fences can be gently rescued.

Grouse

Hills with heather on are grouse hills: Landrover tracks and shooting butts will be seen. Grouse chicks are sensitive to disturbance during the same months as young lambs - mid-March to June. Keep to

THE LOWTHER HILLS

recognised paths and put the dog on the lead. The grouse-shooting season is 12th August to 12th December.

Forestry
Parts of plantations may occasionally be closed off while trees are being felled.

HOW TO USE THIS GUIDE

Grading System

Easy: Tracks and paths. Some may be muddy or rutted. Walking shoes, wellingtons or trainers could be worn.

Moderate: Pathless, but on comfortable ground such as grass without tussocks. Map and compass will normally be carried, and low cloud will bring navigational difficulties - these grassy tops can be featureless. Footwear should be rubber-soled: lightweight walking boots are ideal.

The category also includes some paths that are exposed and narrow above cliffs, or particularly steep.

Hard: Bog, heather, tussocks, rock or scree. A "hard" walk can take up to 50% longer than the same distance and climb on easy ground.

Scrambling

The Southern Uplands are not noted for their scrambling, and such routes as are included are momentary diversions, or of a sort that can only be appreciated by the real enthusiast. Unfrequented scrambles involve dirt, vegetation, loose rock and waterfalls. Situations are romantic, and quite unlike the wide grassy tops. Scrambles are graded for technical difficulty and seriousness.

Grade 1 Difficult rock can be avoided. No exposure. Suitable for inexperienced scramblers (though bad route-finding can sometimes lead to more serious ground).

Grade 2 Some rock may be technically difficult, or above a potentially dangerous drop. Wet climbs, with underwater handholds in streams.

INTRODUCTION

This book includes no Grade 3 scrambling, sadly. (But try lower Lavern Burn GR 904074, and gorge in Ae Forest GR 914986.)

Star Quality
I was going to include a rather poor walk up Comb Law just for those who wanted every two-thousand-foot top. However, Comb Law (Walk 2:2) turned out better than I expected: and so every walk in the book will be found, I hope, enjoyable and worthwhile. However, those with limited time in the area may like to concentrate on those with star gradings. Such gradings are personal - for example, I dislike any road at all in my walks.

* * A walk with no really horrible bits, a natural line, pleasing variety of country and maybe some interesting feature such as a sculpture or a waterfall. A simple walk across rounded hilltops needs some contrasting feature, such as a ravine or riverside, to lift it into this category.
* ** A cracking walk with more than one interesting section. Entertaining enough for children, or for your friends who don't really like walking.
* *** This isn't the Highlands or the Lake District, and we do not have high rocky ridges or classic scrambles.

   There are no *** routes in this book.

Timings and Measurements
A slow walker is still a walker. Arguably, a hillrunner's a walker too. If I supplied timings, then once you'd done a few of the walks you could work out what sort of walker my timings were timed for and adjust accordingly. And if my hypothetical walker was faster than you you'd be upset, and if he was slower you'd be derisive.

So it makes more sense to use the system that applies everywhere. Work out your own speed in terms of distance and the amount of ascent.

IMPERIAL: in terms of tiredness, 1000ft of up is equivalent to 2 miles extra. In terms of time, it's about a mile and a half. Walk 6:1 (Cairnsmore of Fleet) is 6 miles and 2200ft. That'll be about as tiring as $10^{1}/_{2}$ flat miles, and take about as long as 9 miles. After adjusting for the climb, a gentle walker will cover about 2mph, a vigorous one about 3mph. So the Cairnsmore walk will take 3- $4^{1/2}$ hrs, excluding stops.

METRIC: 100m of ascent is worth an extra 1km in terms of tiredness, about 0.7km in terms of time. After making this allowance, a gentle walker covers 3km in an hour, a strong one about 5km. Walk 6:1 (Cairnsmore) has $9^{1/2}$km and 650m: that takes as long as 14km, which will be 3-$4^{1/2}$hrs.

I give altitudes in metres as that's what's on the map. I give distances in both old and new units. I hope, though, that even the most ruthlessly modern walker knows that when I say "100 yds" I also mean "100 metres".

My distances are measured off the map with a little electronic device. Some writers add 5%, 10% or even 20%. This is to cover wiggles or distance up the slope, or just to make the walk longer and more serious. On the Chinese principle of "when in doubt, don't" I've left the distances as they are, so my miles and kilometres are longer than some other people's.

GEOLOGY

The geology of the area is, as geology goes, rather straightforward. Most of the Southern Uplands is made of what a non-geologist will call "ordinary grey rock".

At the beginning of geology, Scotland and England lay on either side of an ocean. There was a deep ocean trench alongside England, and the 'ordinary grey' rock started off as sediments in the bottom of this trench. When the two countries finally collided (the Caledonian Orogeny), these sediments were raised into mountains of Himalayan size. At the same time they were crushed, heated, and so on. However, some of the 'ordinary grey' still shows its sandstone origin, with tiny pebbles of quartz. This grey sandstone is greywacke, and other forms of the ordinary grey are shales and mudstones. All look alike to the casual eye.

As the last remnants of ocean crust were shoved in under the new mountains, friction generated deep underground heat. Bubbles of molten rock rose into the roots of the ordinary grey, and cooled slowly into granite. (If they'd got to the surface they'd have been volcanoes, and cooled rapidly into the quite different rocks of the Lake District.) This granite, grey-speckled white, forms individual mountains quite different from those of the ordinary grey. Criffel, Cairnsmore of Carsphairn, and Cairnsmore of Fleet are dotted with boulders, and rocky-sided. Small mountains indeed, but grim, and with an atmosphere and style all their own.

On its way up, the molten granite heated the surrounding rock, so that various metals turned to hot gas and recondensed higher up. So, in the rocks surrounding the granite, we get the lead, gold and silver that were mined at Wanlockhead and Carsphairn.

Meanwhile the ordinary grey has formed hills that are soft and rounded, but worn by streams into deep vee-shaped cleuchs and linns. In the wide valley of Nithsdale we find, oddly, younger rocks of various complicated sorts, including coal measures. Desert sandstone is seen at Crichope Linn, bright red and crumbly, and utterly different from the mountain greywacke, even if they are both made of sand to start with.

COVENANTERS

After the Reformation, protestantism established itself in Scotland in the particularly austere form associated with Calvin and John Knox. It practised rigorous Old Testament virtues, and among its principles was "presbyterianism": that ministers should be appointed from below, by the congregation and the elders, rather than from above, by a church hierarchy answerable to the King.

During the period of insecurity leading to the English Civil War, King Charles I needed the support of the Presbyterians. He therefore (in 1649) subscribed to their Covenant. After his execution by the English there was even, briefly, a Presbyterian theocracy in Scotland: what might nowadays be called a fundamentalist state. It was overthrown by Cromwell in favour of a more moderate protestantism.

Charles II ("whose word no man relies on") also found it convenient to subscribe to the Covenant, though without any personal belief in its Calvinist principles ("it is not a religion for gentlemen"). Being obliged to listen to six sermons back-to-back before his coronation didn't help.

After the Restoration of 1661 he no longer needed Presbyterian support, and lost no time in overturning the principles of the Covenant. Bishops were restored, ministers were to be chosen by the Church, not the congregation, and ministers appointed since 1649 were required to resign and be reappointed through bishops. Three hundred refused, many of them here in the south-west. They abandoned their manses and held illegal conventicles on the moors.

Persecution was fierce, led by James Graham of Claverhouse (later known as "Bonnie Dundee"). The years from 1678 to 1690 are the Killing Time. Covenanters were shot down on the moors as they attended illegal conventicles, or sent as indentured slaves to the West Indies. The killing was not one-sided. The Archbishop of St Andrews was dragged from his coach and murdered in 1679, and in the same year a force of 250 Covenanters defeated Claverhouse at Drumclog on the Ayrshire/Lanarkshire border.

The kirkyards at Sanquhar (Walk 1:5) and Durisdeer (Walk 2:4) have gravestones of covenanting martyrs. At Sanquhar too is the monument commemorating the Sanquhar Declaration, when the preacher Richard Cameron called for armed insurrection against King and government. A few months later, he died at the battle of Airds Moss. This boggy battlefield is just north of Cumnock, and is overlooked by Walk 7:1. Peden the Prophet, who disguised himself with a mask of cow hide, took refuge in Crichope Linn (Walk 3:5).

Alongside Walk 4:3 is the hilltop grave of two other martyrs, not far from one of the hidden hollows used for conventicles. A covenanting prisoner was rescued in Keltie's Linn (Walk 1:7). Three others escaped in a thunderstorm at Martyr's Knowe (Walk1:5).

After the establishment of the Protestant sovereigns William and Mary the persecutions ceased. The followers of the fiery Richard Cameron became a regiment of the British Army (the Cameronians) and inflicted a defeat on the Jacobite followers of the former Stuart king at Dunbar. When Bonnie Prince Charlie passed through the Enterkin Pass fifty years later, he received a warm welcome at Drumlanrig Castle, but not from the common people of Dumfriesshire.

1: Northern Lowthers

The Lowthers are more contemplative by sunlight, said Dorothy Wordsworth, than other hills are by moonlight. The hills are at their most contemplative seen from the woods of Drumlanrig Castle. Cloud shadows move dreamily over rounded grassy shapes divided by deep little secretive valleys.

Contrariwise, the hills are at their most active when seen from within those secretive valleys. There are three of them. Mennock is where the road goes through to the high mining villages of Leadhills

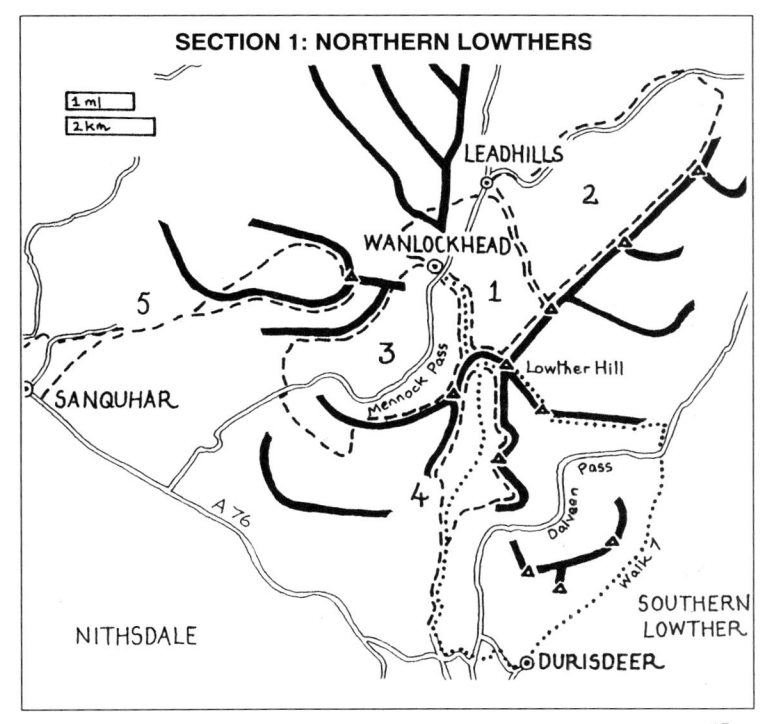

THE LOWTHER HILLS

and Wanlockhead - and a start at 1600ft (500m) certainly brings the tops down to a convenient distance above the car. Dalveen is where the road goes through to Edinburgh and the Scottish Lowlands. In between is Enterkin, where there is no road at all, just the traces of the pony track used by Bonnie Prince Charlie, the Covenanters, and the discerning hillwalker.

The highest hills of the group are decorated with the Civil Aviation Authority's white spheres. They make a striking ornament, and when I came this way after seven non-stop days of hillwalking and found them pink in the sunset, they did suit the mood of that particular moment. It's certainly an unusual experience to walk a tarred road, restricted by 30mph signs, at 2000ft on a bleak plateau with a view stretching 70 miles into the Highlands, Arran and (very, very occasionally) the Paps of Jura. Hill-walking pleasures of a more conventional sort are found between the passes of Enterkin and Mennock. Here is high, steep-sided grass - it's a kind of country found in the Howgills of England, the Ochils, but not anywhere else. The walking is fairly strenuous, but rewarding. East Mount Lowther is such ground, while still offering the technical possibility of the Paps-of-Jura view, and I make no excuse for sending two of the routes in the chapter over this fine small hill.

Walk 1:1
* LOWTHER HILL, GREEN LOWTHER and the MINES:
from WANLOCKHEAD
7¹/₂ miles 1800ft (12km 550m)

When industrial buildings reach a certain age they suddenly turn into fascinating archaeology. This has certainly happened to the ruined mine-workings round Wanlockhead. However, it will be some time yet before the Lowther Domes fall into interesting decrepitude, so that we can start enjoying them. This walk tours two styles of industrial estate: steam and stone by the Wanlock Water, elegant geodesics on the heights.

Guided tours of the mines, underground journey and tea rooms are at the Mining Museum (Easter - October).

MAP: Landranger 78 (Nithsdale) or Harveys Lowther Hills
START/FINISH: Mining Museum, Wanlockhead (GR 874129)

❋ ❋ ❋

NORTHERN LOWTHERS

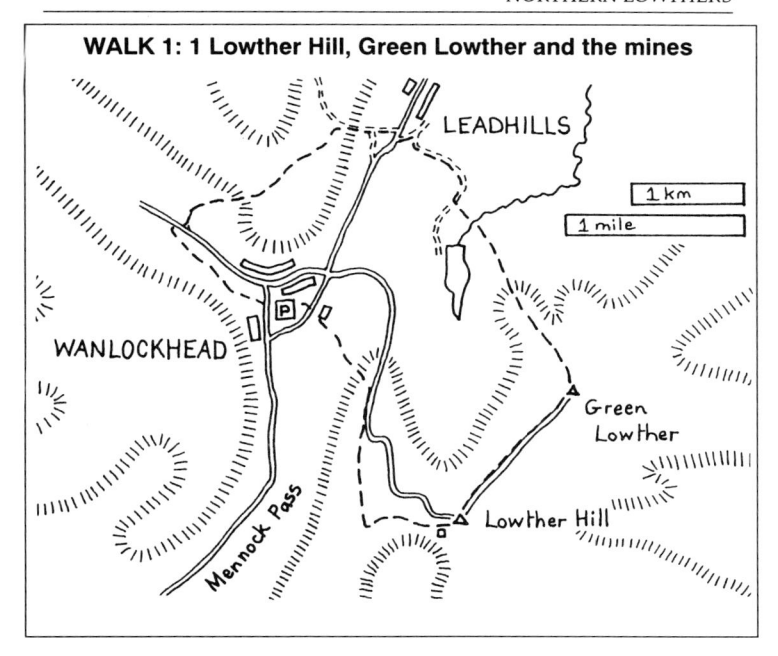

WALK 1: 1 Lowther Hill, Green Lowther and the mines

Cross the road to an SU (Southern Upland) Way sign, and head downstream. The main path follows the old narrow-gauge tramway to left of the water. On the other side are the water-powered beam engine, the mine adits, the ruined smelt mills. The trip into the hill used to be the most fun you could have in Dumfriesshire for 30p. The experience has now been diluted with audio-visual presentations and costs quite a bit more but is still worthwhile.

After half a mile (³/₄km) the valley widens slightly, with a matterhorn-like pile of mine tailings just ahead. This is Glencrieff, the last of the lead mines, that only closed in 1950. The workings are 1600ft (500m) deep - almost down to sea level. Here cross the valley floor on a track, to reach the tarred lane at an SU Way sign. Cross the tarmac to a track just above. This leads round into a narrow stream valley of grass and mine rubble. Here is a final mine, with the remains of one of the world's first steam engines (built in 1789 and

17

THE LOWTHER HILLS

used, like the beam engine further back, to pump water out of the mines).

The little valley is sometimes dry, sometimes has a small stream: note that the water is polluted with lead and is not fit to drink. At the valley's head a wire fence crosses, but can be stepped over at a slight bend, with a larger strainer-post, a few steps up right. The line of the old path is now visible as it contours round the head of the long Snar Valley.

Another wire fence runs down northwards off Wanlock Dod. Again, this can be stepped over (there is also a gate 200yds down left). We now look down the slope to Leadhills. A green track slants down left, continuing the line of the old path. It soon meets a gravel track that slants back right. A fence appears below, and a gate opens onto a green track that wanders down a field to the road. The village of Leadhills, immediately left, has pub, shop and restaurant.

Turn right up the road for 30yds to a track slanting back left. At its top take the track right for 100yds, and fork left to cross the railway at a level crossing. The track crosses the moor, through plenty of old mine remnants and two metal gates. After the second gate, with the reservoir visible ahead, drop left to cross a track below and descend steeply to the Shortcleuch Water.

The slope of Green Lowther beyond is steep and heathery. Fortunately, after the first short rise, the lowest of a line of grouse butts appears just left. From it a small path leads up the butts, and after that the ridge is grassy and easy to the summit. The assortment of radio masts, belonging to BT and various mobile phone companies, are hard to enjoy. We once objected to intrusive concrete trig points - the trig point here is almost lost under one of the steel erections.

However, the road walk along the summit to Lowther Hill is more amusing. We don't often get to walk road at 2000ft (600m) with a view (on a very clear day) to Ben Lawers 80 miles away. And our destination is the exotic puffballs of the Lowther Radar Station. These I find myself able to enjoy although they haven't yet even started to fall into ruins. They belong to the Civil Aviation Authority, and are there to help airliners turn left for New York.

The road enters the CAA's enclosure, passing the summit of the hill which is locked up inside a garage, while walkers pass to the right, outside the enclosure. The road continues down to

NORTHERN LOWTHERS

Wanlockhead, for the late or tired walker; otherwise cross the road top and keep on around the edge of the Dome enclosure, to a descending fence. This goes down slightly north of west, passing the massive metal hut known to walkers as the "Lunch Box", and a stile on the SU Way. (Do not cross the stile, but continue down the fence.) It leads down to the Enterkin Pass, where a low-voltage power line runs across.

The pony track out of the pass leads right, under the power lines, across the steep slope. It joins the radar station road at a hairpin bend. Continue down the road for 300yds, when the SU Way branches down left on a small peaty path. This slants down right, then descends to left of the Walk Inn to the edge of Wanlockhead. Cross the road and go down on earth steps to the car park of the mining museum.

Walk 1:2
ELVAN WATER: LOUISE to LOWTHER
11 ml 2700ft (18km 800m)
Grassy hillsides and tops, gentle railway: moderate

Grassy gentle hilltops, with fences along them: these are typical of the Lowthers. The special feature of this walk is that we get to do 5 miles of them in a straight line, with a quick and easy return along the old railway. The other special feature is the little gap between Louise Wood and White Law: steep heather on one side, steep scree on the other, this is a quarter-mile of mountain ground slipped in among the hills.

Louise Wood has been relabelled on the latest Landranger map as Lousie. But it isn't really that bad! The only other walker I've met in these hills (apart from the SU Way) was on Louise Wood - he claimed it had wider views than the mountains of the Highlands, as well as being easier on the knees!

Leadhills offers various lunches: bar meals at the highest residential hotel in Britain, a licensed cafe with atmosphere and ice creams, and a village shop.

EXTENSIONS: The route can readily be combined with Walk 1:1. A tough diversion after Leadhills is described after the main walk.
MAP: Landranger 78 (Nithsdale) or 71 (Lanark) or Harveys Lowther Hills
Just north of Elvanfoot, turn onto the B7040 (Leadhills & Wanlockhead)

THE LOWTHER HILLS

road. After a mile (1½km), above the abandoned railway bridge, is roadside space for one car. A quarter-mile (½km) further, where the railway line itself crosses, are more spaces.
START/FINISH: Elvan Water viaduct (GR 939173)

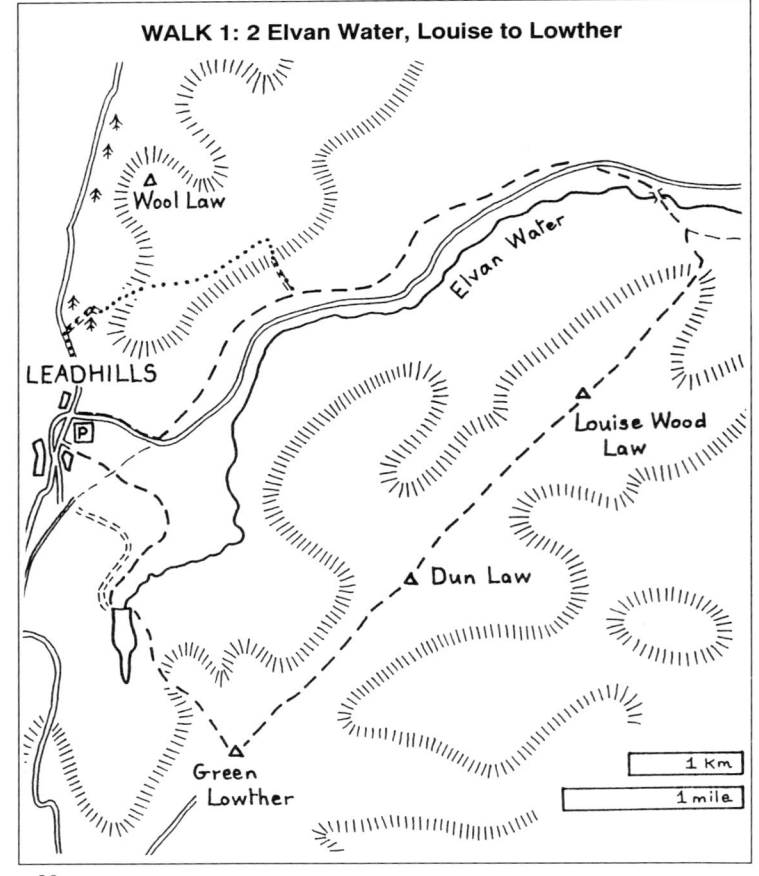

❋ ❋ ❋

WALK 1: 2 Elvan Water, Louise to Lowther

Cross the Elvan Water on the old railway bridge, and continue on the railbed for 200yds, crossing a stile. The driest way now is to turn uphill, alongside and to the right of a square walled enclosure, to a ridgeline fence above. This has a gate slightly right at GR 939163.

Go straight uphill; a fence with broken wall joins from the right. The summit is 50yds away across the fence. From the trig point, the ridge ahead appears short and easy. This illusion is due to two factors. The sharp gap before White Law is concealed; and the Lowther masts, that seem to grow out of the top of Dun Law, are in fact on a hidden hill behind.

Follow the fence southwest: it will guide all the way to Green Lowther. The scree into the first gap is slaty and awkward: there is grass to left of the fence. The following climb may be eased by taking a sheep path that slants out right, passing a tiny outcrop, before turning left to rejoin the fence. White Law is so called because of its grass covering - which appears pale beige in winter - while Dun Law is more heathery. In early summer, the white flowers of the cloudberry decorate the ridge like fresh snow.

Pass between the buildings of Green Lowther to find the trig point under the highest of the radio masts.

Turn northwest, down the long gentle ridge towards Leadhills. As it flattens at the 580m contour, a very worn path can be seen running along its left-hand flank, and this leads down through the heather to the dam of the reservoir. Cross this dam, and take the green track contouring out right from the dam end (not the stony track climbing from the same point). The track runs along above the stream, with a view into the deep empty hollow of the Shortcleuch Water: it's hard to believe that civilisation, in the shape of Leadhills, is only ten minutes away.

The track bends up left to join a wider, stony one. Turn left on this, to cross the moor top. The track crosses the railbed (turn right on this, through a gate marked "Dogs on Leads", to bypass Leadhills). The track leads down into the village, joining the main street as "Horner's Place".

Turn right, through the village, to the road on the right signposted to Elvanfoot. This leads up into a pass and narrow cutting, and here the green track of the former railway strikes up left from the highest point. This leads easily down-valley, with one rude interruption

THE LOWTHER HILLS

where a former viaduct has been dynamited away, leaving a brief descent and climb at a stream.

Uniformly downhill, the final 4 miles should be quick and easy.

VARIANT: The Back of Broad Law
Adds ½ mile 300ft (1km, 100m): hard
Rough heather on almost invisible tracks, this is for the energetic and to be avoided during seasons when grouse are nesting or being shot at.
Follow the main route as far as Leadhills. Take the road northwards out of Leadhills for ½ml (¾km) to where a track climbs right, into a plantation of pine, larch and spruce. At the top of the plantation, the track continues up right, then back left at spoil-heaps of former mining. At its highest point, as it turns back downhill, an old track or path continues straight up - this is only visible as a deep groove in the heather.

It passes above the head of a stream, and continues eastwards across the col between Wool Law and Broad Law. At a red metal gate in a fallen fence, the track becomes clearer. It turns northeast and dips into a second col.

The track starts to climb again, passing between two shaly knolls which are more mine tailings. Here turn off right, to find the first of a series of half-buried grouse-butts. Head just east of south down the line of butts, with a path gradually forming. This becomes a stony track for the final descent to the railway.

Walk 1:3
* Around the MENNOCK PASS
10 miles 2500ft (16km 800m)
Grassy hilltops and valleys, with short sections of heather and tussocks: moderate/hard

---

The Lowther Hills don't mind revealing their innermost secrets to passing motorists. Mind you, the motorist will really need a sun roof to appreciate the high heathery sides of the Mennock Pass. This walk starts low down in that pass, to reach Wanlockhead in time for lunch at the Mining Museum cafe and then return over Auchenlone Hill.

As well as the grassy hilltops, with the wide views or damp mist that we expect in such places, this walk offers little valleys, and the industrial

NORTHERN LOWTHERS

sites of Wanlockhead. Let's not call it dereliction: this is archaeology, for these stony wastes were created in the seventeenth century. Allow an extra hour for the trip into the lead mine. Into a long summer's day you might also squeeze a trip on the Leadhills railway.

So you couldn't find Auchenlone Hill on the map? This use of an old name is a feeble attempt to cover up the fact that this is the first of two routes up East Mount Lowther. Though not the highest this is the best of the Lowther Hills, steep-sided and unindustrialised. By any name, it's a hill worth doing twice.

EXTENSION: Even better is to extend the route to include Walk 1. On this option, the Tracks Cafe (or pub lunch) at Leadhills replaces the cake shop at Wanlockhead's Mining Museum, and the walk grows to 12 miles 3500ft (19km 1100m).

MAP: Landranger 71 (Lanark) or 78 (Nithsdale), or Harveys Lowther Hills

START/FINISH: B797 in the Mennock Pass west of Wanlockhead. A parking area is just north of Glenimshaw (GR 839101)

※   ※   ※

A small stream leads north, away from the road, between high grass slopes. It turns right, to enter a small secret valley. At the head of this, take the right fork of the stream and go up between its low rocky walls - a steep and slightly scrambly ascent. Walk forward over rough heather onto Wether Hill (no cairn).

Continue towards White Dodd, keeping along the top of the steep ground on the right. This gives a grassy sheep path and a view into the hollow of the south-flowing burn, and to the road pass beyond. To reach the unmarked summit of White Dodd you'll have to cross more heather tussocks, though.

The back of White Dodd is grassy again. Keep northeast, and contour the flank of Stood Hill to find a gateway in the fence on the right, leading onto Black Hill. Contour round the head of another deeply-cut stream hollow on the left, and go down Black Hill's north ridge. At the bottom, the Southern Upland Way runs along the embankment of the former light railway through the mine-workings.

Directly opposite is the Wanlockhead Beam engine, a machine for raising water that was itself powered by falling water. The walk

THE LOWTHER HILLS

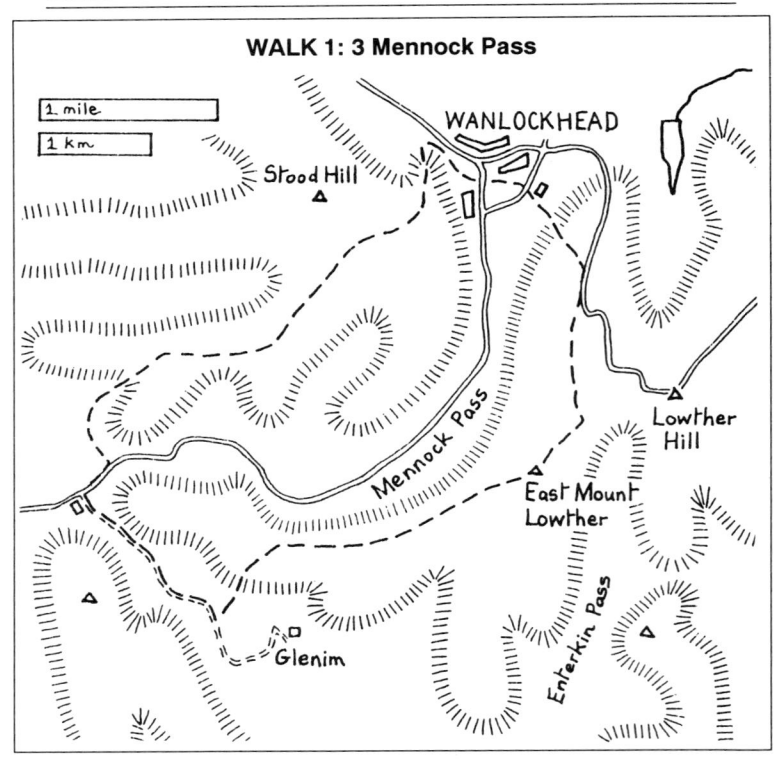

WALK 1: 3 Mennock Pass

[Map showing Wanlockhead, Stood Hill, Mennock Pass, Lowther Hill, East Mount Lowther, Enterkin Pass, and Glenim]

continues to right, but first the archaeology should be explored. You could wander down to the left as far as the tall pointed spoil-heap that has not yet, to my knowledge, been described as the "Matterhorn of Wanlockhead". Alternatively turn up right, along the Southern Upland Way, to the Mining Museum. From here are organised formal tours of the workings and expeditions underground; here also is the tea room.

The SU Way leads on through the car park of the museum and up through Wanlockhead on earthen steps. Cross the B797 at an SU Way signpost, and go up past the once-and-future Wanlockhead Station, and to the right of the crumbling buildings of the Walk Inn.

Once an army barracks and then a rather grim inn, another century of collapse might possibly allow it to join the lead-mines as interesting dereliction. Turn uphill beyond it at two SU Way signs. Follow the waymarked path uphill. After a little wooden footbridge, it runs up to join the access road onto Lowther Hill.

Turn right along the road, and follow it for 400yds to a sharp left-hand bend. Here continue ahead horizontally: note that the SU Way also continues ahead, but slanting uphill. A small grass path leads forward but not upward. Power lines come up to join it as it arrives in the col just north of East Mount Lowther (GR 882105).

This is the Enterkin Pass, an ancient pony-track used by miners, and by Bonnie Prince Charlie on his retreat from England. At the pass turn slightly right, to go up beside the fence onto East Mount Lowther. Or go up onto Auchenlone Hill, if that's the name you prefer. "East Mount Lowther" is amusingly paradoxical: did you notice that it is in fact at the western end of the group?

Descend southwest: this is in the direction indicated by the viewpoint pillar as "Cairnsmore of Fleet". It is not the direction of the fence - those here in mist without a compass will simply have to pick up the viewpoint indicator and carry it with them over the following, tricky section!

The compass-bearing is needed to hit off the narrow grassy neck leading to Threehope Height. (In clear weather, an initial descent west will bring you to quad bike wheelmarks leading to the same point.) Go up Threehope Height, keeping to the right-hand edge for grassy going and deep views.

The descent westwards off Threehope is heathery at first, and quite rough. The obvious continuation over Meikle Snout is heathery, also boggy. Happily, there's a better way. At the foot of the first slope, an old green trackway runs down left, southwest, towards Cock Hill. At stone enclosures near Cock Hill's summit (GR 853087), the track turns southeast towards Glenim. Quicker is to turn right, west, and go down grassy slopes and then steep bracken beside a stream, to reach the Glenim access track.

The track runs out down a deep stream valley. It's an attractive place, with trees above silhouetted against the sunset. Cross the Mennock Water at Glenimshaw house, and turn right up the riverbank alongside the main road to the start-point.

THE LOWTHER HILLS

East Mount Lowther and the top of the Enterkin Pass

Walk 1:4
** Around the ENTERKIN
9 miles 3200ft (15km 950m)
*Grassy hilltops: moderate, but mod/easy if the
steep ascent of Steygail is omitted*

Walking gentle grass along the brinks of deep, waterworn valleys - this is what makes this Dalveen end of the Lowthers so enjoyable. The steep-sided hollow of the Enterkin is beyond the right boot for the whole of the walk. At the Square Nick, the walker can bravely confront one of the steepnesses head-on, or else slide away gratefully by a dry valley into the sheltered bottom of the hollow.

MAP: Landranger 78 (Nithsdale)
A tarred farm lane runs north from Muiryhill farm. After a mile it bends left for Inglestone farm, while a grass track with a Scottish Rights of Way Society sign runs forward. There is verge-parking at the junction.

START/FINISH: Muiryhill track junction (GR 874046)

✵ ✵ ✵

NORTHERN LOWTHERS

The SRWS sign "Enterkin Pass" indicates the way northward along the track. This runs between fences and through several gates, with views through a grown-out hedge to the wooded hollow of the Enterkin Burn. After ½ml (¾km) it emerges into open pasture, to continue northwards as a grass shelf high above the burn.

The track ends at a cluster of sheep-handling pens. Follow the ridgeline fence north over a grass hummock into a col (GR 877064). Now an old grass track, reinforced by the wheelmarks of the

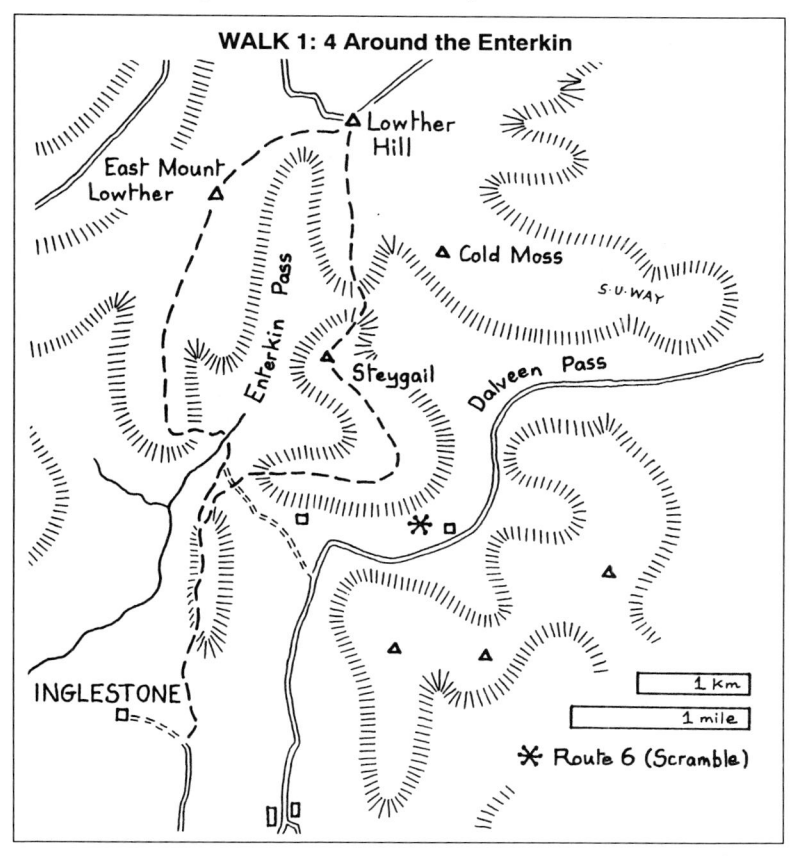

WALK 1: 4 Around the Enterkin

Lowther Hill
East Mount Lowther
Enterkin Pass
Cold Moss
S·U·WAY
Steygail
Dalveen Pass
INGLESTONE

1 km
1 mile

✱ Route 6 (Scramble)

THE LOWTHER HILLS

modern quad bike, slants gently down the left-hand slope. Follow this to a gate (GR 876073). Walk through the gate to join a well-surfaced track at a zigzag. The track leads downhill, through a gate and then bending left and fording the Enterkin Burn. It starts to slant up around the low shoulder of Thirstane Hill. At a gate across the track, 200yds after the ford, turn uphill to right of a fence.

Continue uphill on pathless grass. Views behind are all the length of Nithsdale, with Criffel blocking off the end and, on a clear day, Lake District hills peeping round Criffel's shoulders.

Walk northwards along the grassy plateau, keeping close to the right-hand edge for views across the deep valley of the Enterkin Pass to Steygail. Assess the steepness of Steygail's northern slope: this you will be confronting on the homeward leg.

A fence running in from the left indicates that the summit is near. The summit itself is decorated with the pillar of a viewpoint indicator. Southwards, "Scafell 3210'" is a mistake - that's the height of Scafell Pike - and northwards, "Ben Cruachan 97mls" may be an inflated claim. However, I can personally confirm the Paps of Jura at 92 miles, while Ben More and Ben Lomond will be easily picked out on any crisp winter's day when the Highland hills have snow on them and sun shining on that snow.

Descend a grassy path to left of the fence to the col of the Enterkin Pass (GR 882106, recognisable by the power line passing through). If time is short, or weather unpleasant, the shorter and more sheltered return is by this pass. Simply follow the small path under the power lines, and then the stream. This short-cut is only slightly less good than the full route.

Continue uphill to left of the fence on a grassy path that makes it unnecessary to transfer to the tarred road that climbs beside you on the left. Also on the left are the Mercury transmission towers, and ahead are the white spheres of the Civil Aviation Authority's radar. Keep eyes on the fine view down the Enterkin Pass, to avoid beholding this high-altitude industrial estate.

Fifty yards short of the domes, a stile on the right is marked by SU Way waymarks. Cross the stile to pass a small metal hut, known as the "Lunch Box" for its usefulness as sandwich-eating shelter during blizzards. SU Way waymarks and a small path lead round the flank of the hill to a second stile. Cross this, and turn downhill beside the fence for 400yds only. Here the fence, and the SU Way, bear left. Recross the fence and continue south down a wide grassy ridge. Note that you are seeking a very precise point at the tip of this ridge, with steep slopes on either hand. In mist, this will call for accurate compass work.

The ridge narrows at its tip, and a short steep descent drops into the Square Nick. This is the dramatic little pass at GR 892087, separating Steygail from the rest of the mountain mass. The grass slope ahead appears, from here, vertical. From Thirstane Hill, earlier in the walk, it was clearly no worse than 45°. Measurement off the map spoils it all by revealing only 30°.

If you don't fancy the slope ahead, or if your shoes are flat-soled ones and the grass is wet, you can avoid Steygail. Turn right (west), to descend the dry stream bed to the Enterkin Burn. Go down beside the burn to rejoin the outward route at the ford.

Otherwise, ascend the steep slope to the summit of Steygail. This has fine new views into the Dalveen Pass. The one gentle slope of this upstanding hill is used for the descent.

Follow wheelmarks southeast, gently downhill. At the 500m contour, a small col lies before a slight rise in the ridge: from this col contour out right on wheelmarks, around the head of Glenvalentine. The path gains the crest of the narrow grass spur on the left, and this leads down westward.

At the spur's foot, a track climbs up from Dalveen Farm. Walk to right, along the track, for a few yards, to pass its highest point and go through a gate. Turn left, and walk south along the top of the slope with fence on your left. Go through a small gate (sheep-width, not tractor-width), and then step over a low double fence - the second half is electric, not usually switched on. Continue southwards over two grassy hummocks, to the col at GR 877064. Here the outward route is rejoined; a gate at the top of the facing slope marks the start of the fence that guides you south to the track end $^{1}/_{4}$ mile ($^{1}/_{2}$km) further on.

THE LOWTHER HILLS

Walk 1:5
SANQUHAR to STOOD HILL
13¹/₂ miles 2600ft (22km 800m)
Paths and grassy hilltops: moderate

This is a straightforward walk of grassy ridges over pleasantly rounded hills. What would be tough and tussocky ground is tamed by quad bike wheelmarks which give easy going over most of the circuit.

The hills lie back from Sanquhar, with a couple of miles of gently-rising sheep fields before the uplands. These 2 miles give us, at the start of the walk, a rocky riverbank: and at the end, a homeward romp along the Southern Upland Way. It's nice to descend onto a town at evening, and get to the pub before we get to the car - it's also nice to leave the car at home, and get to the walk by train. However, the route can be started from the junction near Bogg farm, to shorten it by 4 miles (7km). There's room to park at the ruin (GR 800115), a few yards up left from the road end.

EXTENSIONS: The walk can also be extended to include the mines and village of Wanlockhead, pinching part of Walk 1. (This variant is described after the main walk.)

MAP: Landranger 71 (Lanark) or 78 (Nithsdale)

START/FINISH at Macmillan Square, Sanquhar. This is just north of the A75 at the west end of the town, and is reached by a forking side road from the conspicuous eighteenth-century Council House. (The square is reached from the railway station by walking 300yds downhill.) GR 779101

❋   ❋   ❋

Walk northwest past the church, using a footpath to left of the road at first. At Crawick cross the footbridge to the B740 and turn right, uphill, under the railway viaduct. After 500yds a track forks off right: an ancient sign prohibits unauthorised vehicles. A smaller sign warns of a dog, which may jump out suddenly from a garage on the right.

Pass in front of a cottage onto a path through trees, which leads to the riverbank. Our route crosses the fine high footbridge, but a path ahead, beyond the picnic site, can be explored up the riverbank for 200yds before returning to the footbridge.

NORTHERN LOWTHERS

Cross, and head up the east bank of the Crawick. Here it forms the "Sodgers' Pool", named after the French prisoners of war who bathed here at the time of Napoleon. After 200yds the path crosses a smaller footbridge over a side stream. Here the path for the hills doubles back uphill to the right. First, however, wander on over the footbridge for another 300yds to a wooden bench. Here is the "Witches' Pool", where the rocky banks overhang excitingly.

Return to the smaller footbridge, and take the path that slopes uphill with occasional wooden steps to the corner of the hill road at GR 784112. Turn left up the road for a mile (1½km) to the T-junction at the small ruin near Bogg (the starting point for the shorter version of the walk).

Here turn right, towards Bogg, but at once fork left onto the

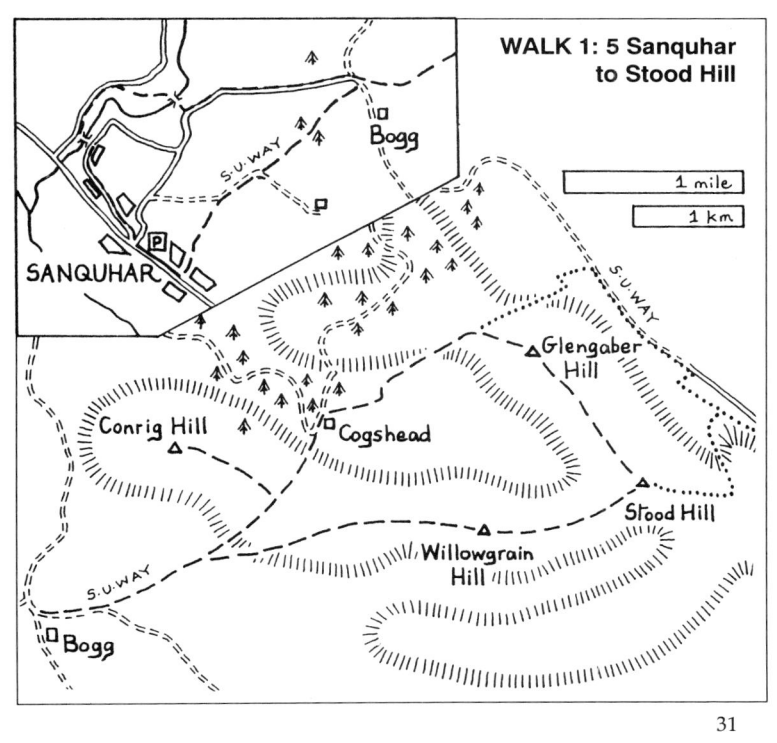

THE LOWTHER HILLS

upper track. After nearly half a mile (600m) the track bends right towards a plantation, and here a waymark pole on the left indicates a small path. Head up the gentle ridge to a ladder stile, and continue uphill, soon with a fence on the right. The path, which is the Southern Upland Way, becomes clearer as it steepens, with a stile at the skyline ridge.

A pleasant diversion can now be made to Conrig Hill. Do not cross the stile ahead, but follow the fence to the left - quad bike marks make the going even easier. This grassy eminence has its very own trig point, and a view down a steep drop towards the Cog Burn. Return along the fence to the stile at the Southern Upland Way. The route will follow this for the next 2 miles (3km).

The SU Way descends a grassy slope beside a dry valley. A knoll on the right is the Martyr's Knowe. Here three Covenanters captured by the Laird of Drumlanrig made their escape during a sudden and providential thunderstorm. The path turns back left to a stile onto a forest road. Turn right, and enter the forest briefly, to a signpost on the right at a gate. A notice here asks for "minimal intrusion" during April and May, when lambs and grouse chicks are being born.

The Way runs to left of the enclosures at Cogshead, then slants uphill on an old grass path. Despite National Trail status, this is now so little used that in mist it is hard to trace among the sheep paths, and a compass-bearing will help get you from one waymark to the next. After 600yds come two small footbridges and a stile, and now the path has been built up with rubble and clay, and is easily followed. The upper Cog is a grassy hollow among the hills where sheep are the only signs of man: one of the better bits of the SU Way. It rises to a stile beside Glengaber Hill. (Here the Wanlockhead extension heads on down to the Wanlock Water.)

Don't cross the stile, but head right, alongside the fence, over Glengaber Hill and then more steeply onto Stood Hill. At a T-junction of fences, a gate on the left lets you through to the grassy summit with its small pools. And in one of the pools, an upstanding rock: it slightly resembles the one at the summit of Haystacks in the Lake District.

Go past the summit for 50yds to an old iron gate, and double back along the far side of the fence on more quad bike wheel-marks.

Descending from Lowther Hill towards East Mount Lowther (Walk 1:3)
In the Square Nick (Walk 1:7)

Steygail, East Mount Lowther and Lowther Hill (seen from Well Hill, Walk 2:5)
The Dalveen Pass (sections 1 & 2)

NORTHERN LOWTHERS

The col before Willowgrain is a hidden inner knee-joint of the hills. Stream-carved slopes fold out from here, and some of them are fairly steep. Including the one up onto Willowgrain Hill itself, which is now to be climbed. (The flanking path marked on Landranger above the Glendyne Burn is no longer visible on the ground.)

Cross through the fence on the crest of Willowgrain. The backslope is rough heather, but gently downhill. On the climb to the nameless 486m top a gate lets you back to the left-hand side. A fence-bend marks the obscure summit. Now leave the faithful fence and keep ahead, westward, down tussocky grass. Go through a fence gate beside the Shiel Burn at the 350m contour, and immediately cross the stream itself below its small gorge. Contour west without further loss of height to the fence alongside the SU Way. The fence leads down to a gate that lets you through onto the waymarked footpath.

Return down the SU Way, across the ladder stile to the Brandleys farm track. Just past where the lower track from Bogg joins, take a stile on the left. Head across the field to low footbridges and a stile - this straightening of the SU Way is so recent that a path has not yet formed. A stile leads into a plantation, and a kissing gate leads out again at the back. The built-up path leads southwest, to join the gravel farm track from Lochside. Where this turns right, keep ahead on a path with benches to rest on. Pass under the railway to meet the main street of Sanquhar.

Turn right along the street. You pass first the obelisk marking the signing of the Sanquhar Declaration in 1680. "If you would know the nature of their crime, then read the story of that killing time." Then you come to the Oldest Post Office in Great Britain. At the end of the street, in an early example of a traffic calming measure, the fine "Council House" of Robert Adam projects into the A76. Two pubs and a tea-room complete the amenities of central Sanquhar.

Bear right just beyond the Council House to the starting point.

EXTENDED VERSION to WANLOCKHEAD
15 miles 2000ft (24km 900m)
Two sorts of people won't want to drop to the Wanlock Water along the

THE LOWTHER HILLS

furthest leg of Walk 1:5. First, those who think Walk 5 is quite long enough already. Second, those who intend to take in the interesting lead-mines and village by way of Walk 1:1 (Lowther Domes). We could add a third category: those who don't like to interrupt their walk with cream cakes and a cup of tea at the Mining Museum - but who would be included in that final category?

Follow Walk 1:5 to the stile beside Glengaber Hill and cross this stile, thus remaining on the SU Way. Its green track descends in zigzags to cross the Wanlock Water at a footbridge. Turn right up the dusty track, which can soon be left in favour of the railbed of a narrow-gauge railway on the right. Continue past the ruined mine cottages and the remains of a Beam Engine - a pump for raising water, itself powered by falling water.

The path (still the SU Way) enters the village at the lead-mining museum. Here the various structures are explained, and you can book a trip into the side of the hill, where glassfibre miners are working a 24hr day in the dark.

Return for $^1/_4$ mile ($^1/_2$km), to take the steep little stream valley on the left. This climbs southwards onto the col behind Black Hill. Go through a fence gate (GR 866125) to find a vague track leading up alongside the fence to the iron gate just before the summit of Stood Hill. Come back through this gate to continue alongside the fence towards Willowgrain Hill on the main walk.

Walk 1:6
STEYGAIL SCRAMBLE
See map for walk 1:4
This direct route up Steygail gives a good but very short scramble (grade 1).

START: Toll Cottage, in the Mennock Pass (A702) (GR 900068)

Go through the track gate on the west side of the road, and take the lesser, left-hand track. This leads to the bank of the burn, which is crossed. The stream gully directly opposite is the route of ascent.

Go through a gate a few yards left of the stream, then enter its grassy slot. In summer, thistles and nettles guard the entrance. In winter, I was alarmed by the debris of the very small avalanche.

NORTHERN LOWTHERS

Around the 300m contour the gully becomes rocky. A steep narrow chimney is climbed on good holds. At the top, the stream divides. The right-hand fork gives a little more scrambling. Continue upstream onto open slopes. Once on the grassy plateau above, Steygail's final grassy cone is a short stroll to the northwest.

It seems to me that those prepared to tackle so high and steep a slope, not to mention the nettles, thistles and small avalanche, for the sake of so short a scramble, will probably not appreciate or need a particular walk of 2, 7½ or even 20 miles (3-30km) to continue on. One short and interestingly rough option is to descend into the Square Nick, just north of Steygail, and then into the deep Dinabid Lane. A longer round would take in Lowther Hill before descending to Upper Dalveen. This descent should not be from Cold Moss, but rather from Comb Head, further down the ridge.

Or you could go right down this ridge, over Laght Hill and across the A702, to take in some of the territory of Section 2 and finish with a descent of the Toll Cottage Cleuch (Walk 2:3).

Walk 1:7
** ENTERKIN and WELL PASSES
17 miles 3600ft (27km 1100m)
Path and grassy track, 1½ miles of minor road: easy
See overview map for section 1 (p15)

This walk uses long-distance paths ancient and modern to visit much of what's best in the Lowthers. The Enterkin Pass is a spectacular little stream slot, long used as the shortest if not the easiest approach to Wanlockhead from the south. The small gorge at its foot is 'Keltie's Linn'. Covenanting prisoners were being led through this pass towards trial in Edinburgh. (Covenanters were held and then executed in Greyfriars Kirkyard, today noted more for its statue of a little dog called Greyfriars Bobby. The luckier ones were merely sent as indentured slaves to the plantations in the West Indies.) An ambush and rescue took place in the Linn: Keltie was the guard who was shot. Fifty years later, Bonnie Prince Charlie used this route on his return from Derby. In the autumn of 1745, it was still a long hard march from here to the field of Culloden.

The lovely village of Durisdeer is the half-way point. Next is the Well Pass, which is the one the Romans used. Their small fort finds a new role in the modern world as a storage-point for black plastic bags of silage. The less ancient coaching-road gives a gentle grassy ascent below these neatly-folded hills.

The Southern Upland Way, a splendid-looking line across the map of Scotland, turns out on the ground to have rather too much forest road and bleak bits. The crossing of Lowther Hill is one of its high points geographically, and also one of its better bits of walking.

This walk can equally be started at Durisdeer, while those who have the opportunity to incorporate a Durisdeer tea into the day will start at Overfingland (small lay-by at the foot of the SU Way GR 928094). While the two narrow passes and one high ridge combine into a very satisfying walk, the seriously energetic will refer to the overview maps for sections 1 and 2, and incorporate Walks 1:4 and 2:4 to make an arduous route that's hills all the way.

MAP: Landranger 78 (Nithsdale) or Harveys Lowther Hills

START/FINISH: Wanlockhead Lead Mining Museum (GR 873129)

* * *

From the end of the car park SU Way waymarks lead uphill, across the main road and up to right of the Walk Inn. The hill path rises to join the Lowther Domes access road. Turn right along this for just 400yds, to a hairpin left bend. Here continue ahead and level (not ahead and rising, on the SU Way). Power lines join from below as you reach the Enterkin Pass (GR 882107).

The small path follows the power lines down the deep stream slot, to cross steep slopes above the small gorge of Keltie's Linn. The valley floor levels and you have to jump over the stream a few times before the old path reappears a little way up the left-hand slope. The path runs out onto track at the foot of Glenvalentine.

Turn left up the track, through a gate, and at the first left-hand bend keep ahead to pass above stone field-walls to a gate. The old path slants up left, to reach the ridge-crest above at a small col (GR 877065). Walk south over a knoll to the next col, to find a track running south. This crosses the top of the high grassy slope above the wooded Enterkin Burn, then becomes a hedged lane passing to right of plantations. It runs down to the tarred entrance road of Inglestone farm.

After a mile (1½km), turn left at a junction to descend in steep

NORTHERN LOWTHERS

zigzags to the main road. Turn left for 200yds, crossing the Carron Water, and then right, onto another minor road. After ¼ mile (½km), opposite a small wood on the right, a rough track turns off left to reach a parallel road higher up. Turn right, to cross a ford with footbridge alongside and reach Durisdeer. Here is a phone box, a cold-water tap, and, on Sunday afternoons in July, August and September, a sumptuous home-baked tea in the hall above the church. That seventeenth-century church is attractively set among trees, overlooked by Black Hill. Round the back is a set of tombstones as sumptuous and sugary as the Durisdeer Church teas, with marble angels and barley-sugar columns.

Durisdeer

Pass to right of the church onto the track up the Well Pass. The second gate on the left leads to a lesser, muddier track if you want to visit the Roman fortlet: a wall stile further up-valley lets you regain the main track. Otherwise, keep on that main track, up the right-hand side of the valley, on the smooth grass of the old coach road (known locally as the Well Path). Sandstone gateposts mark the crossing of the pass.

The track continues, deeply rutted on the Lanarkshire side of the pass. After another 1½ miles (2km), ignore a track on the right and pass along the left-hand edge of a plantation onto the main A702.

The Roman road is somewhere under the soggy grass above the road, but simpler is to turn right along the road's verge to the SU Way signpost just before Overfingland. The SU Way manages to make the long climb to Lowther Hill even longer by including two sharp descents on the way up. The clear, waymarked path is accompanied by a fence and has little wooden bridges here and there (but not everywhere - there's a boggy bit on the very first climb).

Three elegant glassfibre domes decorate the summit. Sidelit by a setting sun the structures have a striking simplicity of form, even though one might wish them to have that simplicity somewhere other than the highest point of Dumfriesshire. The SU Way circles left just below the dome enclosure to descend alongside the access road, while short-cutting its zigzags. At the 580m contour, its waymarks drop left, on the hill path that started our walk.

2: Southern Lowthers

The Dalveen Road is a modern and artificial division of the Lowthers. South of the pass, the contemplative tops continue, and here is a fourth steep-sided pass to add to Mennock, Enterkin and Dalveen. The Romans had a road through Well Pass, and have left behind a small earthen fort. In the seventeenth century the Well Pass carried the coach-road to Edinburgh. Today that coach road is another fine walkers' route into, or out of, the hills.

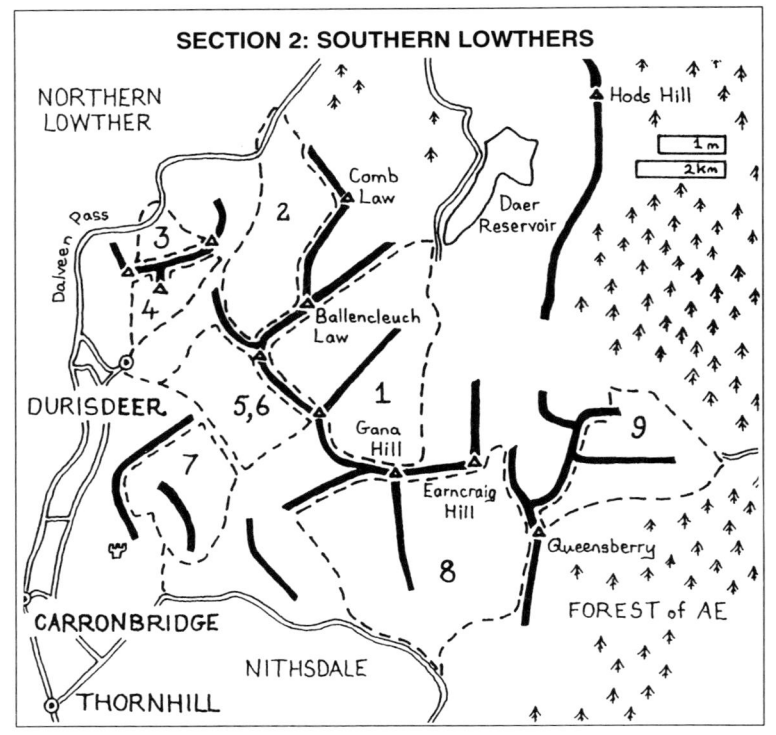

SECTION 2: SOUTHERN LOWTHERS

SOUTHERN LOWTHERS

At the foot of the pass lies the village of Durisdeer, its grey church tower emerging from the trees at the foot of Black Hill. Durisdeer is the most attractive start-point in this book, made still more so on Sunday afternoons of July, August and September when home-baked teas are offered in the room above the church.

The most interesting hills of the group lie between here and Dalveen, with the Well Hill group, not quite reaching 2000ft/610m, being better than the surrounding higher hills.

A Landrover track runs over Scaw'd Law and Wedder Law, rendering them slightly too motorised for many hillwalkers. At 2000ft/610m exactly, Earncraig is distinguished as the lowest hill in Scotland, or at least in Donald's Tables. Queensberry, the highest and southernmost, projects as a viewpoint into the Dumfriesshire plain.

Walk 2:1
GANA HILL, BALLENCLEUCH LAW from DAER RESERVOIR
10 miles 2500ft (16km 750m)
Track and grassy slopes: moderate

Here we walk the watershed between Solway and Atlantic; Daer is one of the sources of the Clyde. The rounded hills lie back from the water, and the reservoir shows little in the way of reflections. Come expecting prettiness, and you'll be disappointed. 'Bleak' is the word for Daer, with the promise of wide empty country ahead to walk over.

Kirkhope is pronounced "Kirkup", and Daer is "Dar".

MAP: Landranger 78 (Nithsdale) or Harveys Lowther Hills

START/FINISH: head of Daer Reservoir (GR 965060). Parkable verges before the track end of Crookburn; but don't obstruct entrance to the farm

❄   ❄   ❄

A track leads southwards past the shepherd's cottage of Kirkhope. It passes above the abandoned house at Daerhead. The valley of Daer Water closes in, while the lumpy shapes of Gana and Earncraig hills lend shape to the scenery.

After 2 miles (3km) the track starts to swing right and uphill.

THE LOWTHER HILLS

WALK 2: 1 Gana from Daer

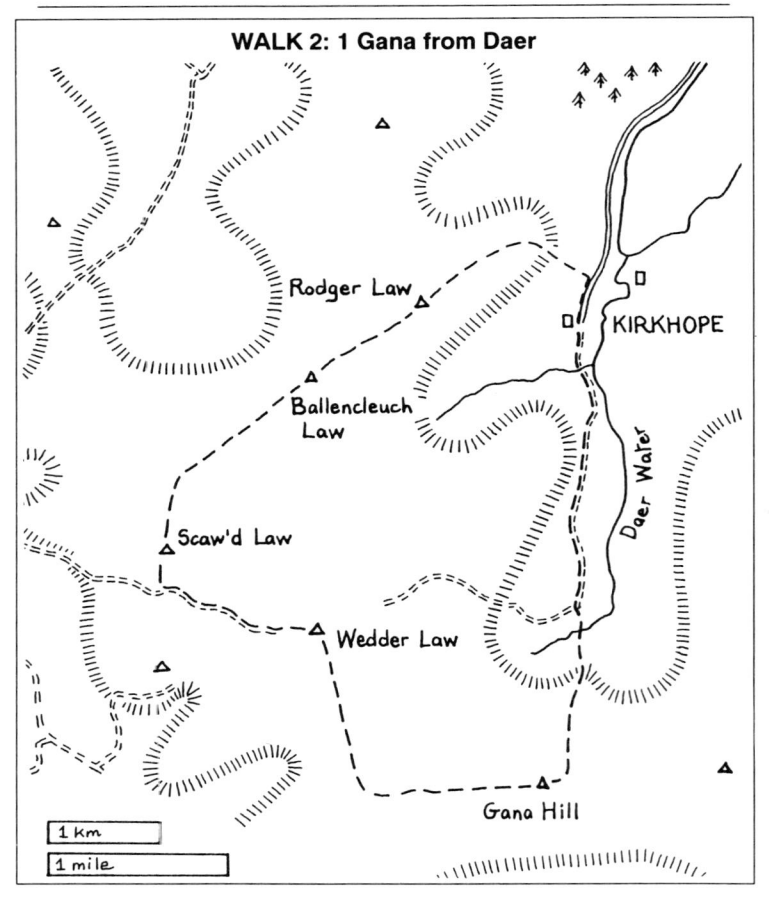

Here go ahead on wheelmarks to cross the Thick Cleuch stream and pass to left of some stone-walled enclosures. A gateway in the fence beyond (GR 961023) and the crossing of the tiny Gana Burn lead to the foot of Gana's northern spur. The spur is a pleasant grassy ascent with a sheep path. As you climb, the bulk of Queensberry fills the view on the left. Over its right shoulder you may see the Solway

SOUTHERN LOWTHERS

Firth, with Skiddaw rising beyond.

You reach the crest at a fence corner 200yds east of Gana's summit. At your feet, the V-shaped hollow of the Kenriva Burn leads the eye southwards across the dark hills of the Forest of Ae to Criffel. It's a sheltered lunch-spot on a windy day. Walk right, up the fence, to the first summit cairn. 400yds further along the fence is the second summit cairn, which is to south (left) of the fence and offers new views of Nithsdale. At some undefined point between the two cairns was the summit of Gana.

The fence leads on westward, with a gate opposite the spur to Garroch Fell allowing the walker back to its northern, right-hand side (GR 946011). Go down beside the fence into the boggy col. At the top end of a stone wall leading down left, a gateway lets you back onto the left-hand (west) side of the fence. For driest ground cross the second, slightly lower, col at its highest point. This is well to left of the fence. Rejoin the fence to ascend Wedder Law.

Donald-baggers using Harveys map should note that Wedder Law is 672m, not 666m as marked. It is therefore higher than the outlying Shiel Dod. The actual summit is not marked in any way, and is 50yds east of the fence - a gate allows access. Return through the fence and head west to find the top of a stony Landrover track. Yes, Wedder Law is one of the five Donalds with vehicle access to the summit. Accordingly, it is occasionally leapt off by paraglidists. The track itself is uncomfortable walking, but its ditches have dried out the grass alongside to give an easy descent. It crosses the col at a small stream, offering useful drinking water.

The main walk continues along the track to a gate. However, keen Donald-baggers can leave the track here, crossing rough ground westward to the summit of Glenleith Fell. This is a truly unworthy Donald top, only 8ft (2½m) above the qualifying height and with just 69ft (21m) of rise after the col. From its tiny, quartz-topped cairn, return northwards alongside a fence. The ground is rough peat and heather, further harshened by loose remnants of a previous fence. Rejoin the non-baggers at a gate on the track on the slope of Scaw'd Law (GR 924032).

Go through the gate and up alongside the fence to join the stone wall across the summit. Personal observation contradicts both Landranger and Harveys, suggesting the northern summit is the

41

THE LOWTHER HILLS

higher by 2m.

Pass through the wall at a gap, and go on grass alongside a fence to Ballencleuch Law and then, without fence, to Rodger Law. As well as its trig point, Rodger Law is decorated with an anemometer pole and weather measuring station. Planning permission for a wind farm on this conspicuous hill has been refused, and we can hope that this pole, and the one on Watchman's Brae beyond, will soon be cleared away. Go down the gentle ridge to that second pole, and descend east, keeping to left of fenced ground, to reach the road at the head of the reservoir.

Walk 2:2
COMB LAW
8 miles 1900ft (13km 550m)
Grassy hilltops: moderate

This is the kind of rough, flat ridgewalking that gives the Lowthers a bad name. This walk is included so as to give those who want to do every Donald a way up Comb Law. Comb Law could be the least exciting of the 144 Donald tops. Too rough for fast walking, not rough-hagged enough to be an ordeal and adventure, it's hard to see how this nondescript hill got itself an outlier with the enticing title of Meikle Shag.

But then again, it has to be said that Comb Law has a small pond surrounded by cloudberry flowers, while Black Law SW Top - a Donald in the Manor Hills and so not in this book - has no redeeming feature whatsoever. And besides, to attempt such absolute comparisons is to stray from the fence line of the walk into the deep bog of logical contradiction: for being the most boring is itself a slightly interesting quality...

So we abandon all attempts at the dullest possible walk by continuing onto pleasant walkable grass at Ballencleuch Law, while the final descent into the Well Pass is enjoyably wild and stony.

MAP: Landranger 78 (Nithsdale) or Harveys Lowther Hills

START/FINISH: lay-by at Nether Fingland, where the Southern Upland Way off Lowther Hill reaches the A702 (GR 929093)

❊   ❊   ❊

SOUTHERN LOWTHERS

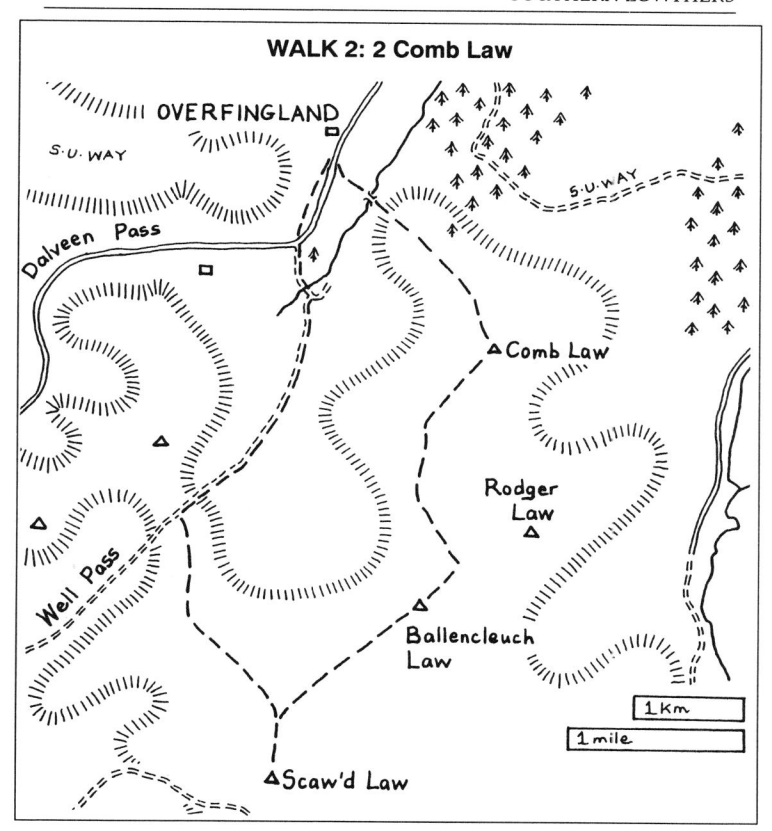

WALK 2: 2 Comb Law

A footbridge crosses the Portrail Water: to work out where, stand at the road side and trace the cattle tracks back down the face of Meikle Shag. These tracks make the steepish slope to Meikle Shag fairly easy.

Cross the col beyond, on fairly rough grass, above the corner of a forest. Follow a fence to the top of Comb Law. The summit is marked only by a fence junction. Follow one of these fences southwest to Hirstane Rigg. The flat-topped ridge mixes heather and grass,

43

THE LOWTHER HILLS

with flowers of cloudberry in May and June. Hirstane Rigg has a nicely-built cairn. Climb gently south onto Ballencleuch Law.

The grass is now short, allowing enjoyable fast progress along the fence to Scaw'd Law. The summit of this is indeterminate, and for the purpose of this walk can be taken to be where fence meets wall at the north end of the plateau. Follow the wall northwest then north to Durisdeer Hill, and down steep grassy slopes to the Well Pass at the top of the Roman Road.

Follow the track to the right, back into Lanarkshire. Where it forks, bear left, to cross a stream and then bend back right and pass to the left of a plantation. The track reaches the A702 $^3/_4$ mile (1km) south of the start-point. To left of the motor road, the old Roman one is heather-grown but can be used to complete the walk.

Walk 2:3
* LAVERN BURN with descent of TOLL COTTAGE CLEUCH
3 miles 1300ft (5km 400m)
Stream bed scrambling: grade 1
** Variant: ascent of TOLL COTTAGE CLEUCH only

Two straightforward stream scrambles make a short but enjoyable circuit. There is potential for more serious scrambling in the lower Lavern Burn. The variant without the Lavern Burn is rather easier but still good, and is described separately below.

MAP: Landranger 78 (Nithsdale) or Harveys Lowther Hills

START/FINISH at bridge over Lavern Burn on the spectacular Dalveen Pass road (GR 903074)

❋   ❋   ❋

The stream is a series of waterfalls in a wooded hollow. These waterfalls are too serious for our present purposes, so go up steep grassy slopes to left (north) of the stream. Near the top the slope becomes broken, with some stone, scree and rock. Below this rough ground, traverse right towards the stream. Pass immediately below the topmost one of the streamside trees, to join the stream.

Here you are above the main waterfalls, as the stream runs

SOUTHERN LOWTHERS

WALK 2: 3 Lavern Burn and Toll Cottage Cleuch

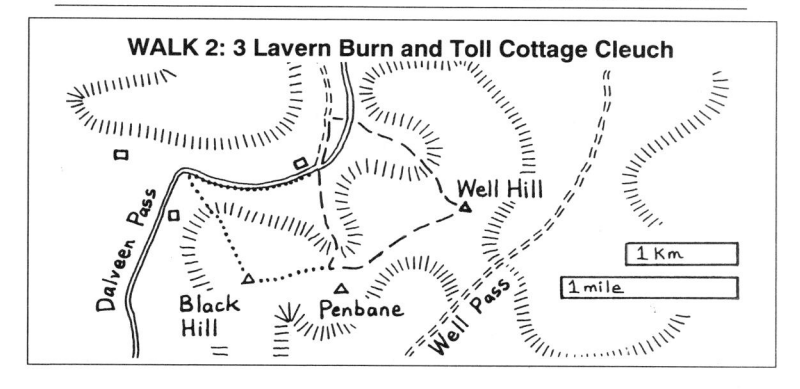

down out of a little valley. Advance upstream, to find a 6ft (2m) fall. The green mossy wall to left of the main stream looks most unattractive. However, feel around among the moss to find sound rock and several incut handholds. The pitch is thus surmounted with ease and some astonishment.

Walk up two short cascades. Now the stream narrows between low vertical walls. You can ascend the rib of rock and grass on the left onto open slopes. Alternatively, a slightly more challenging route, you can proceed along the narrow part with a foot on each wall to a final waterfall. A messy slope of grass and scree to left of the fall has enough rock poking through to allow an ascent.

Walk up the high hidden valley above, alongside the stream. It is moderately tussocky. At the head of the valley the stream forks at a circular sheep fank. Go straight up the slope above the fank to the summit of Well Hill. This is a satisfying summit - except to Donald-baggers, as it's 1988ft (606m) high.

Fence and broken wall lead southwest, with a bend to the right on the way down. At the wall end the fence continues, and skirts the south-eastern slope of a slight rise in the ridge before dropping to the stream head north of Penbane.

The fence rises slightly to a gate (GR 902058), and here you leave it to descend northwards with the stream. The stream banks close in and become slightly rocky. (The route used in the reverse direction, to come up the Toll Cottage Cleuch, is the ridge to the right; but this

THE LOWTHER HILLS

is hard to find in descent, and the steep grass above the rocks can be awkward coming downhill.)

The stream steepens, and you find yourself looking down a waterfall into a small grassy hollow. This is the left-hand one of two waterfalls descending into the hollow: between the two falls is a rocky rib. Return upstream for 10yds, and go up a slanting shelf to the crest of the rocky rib. Descend on the other side to the top of the other waterfall.

From the top of this fall, traverse right, across the top of a rocky slope, just below a small tree. Descend a mixture of rock and scree into the rocky hollow.

Go down the stream below, keeping close to the water - it is easy to traverse out sideways and end up perched on a high grassy slope. Two short waterfalls on the way down can be descended or avoided.

The stream reaches the road at Toll Cottage. Cross onto the access track for Upper Dalveen and follow this up the flat valley bottom. Go up to the Lavern Burn: the road can be regained immediately to left of the high concrete culvert, or the culvert itself can be entered by a wet and rather exposed scramble.

** VARIANT: TOLL COTTAGE CLEUCH: ascent only
3 miles 1000ft (5km 300m)
Stream scramble: grade 1

*The ascent of the cleuch is not difficult, and takes the scrambler into some fine situations in the heart of the hill. However, the return to the start-point involves the descent of a high and very steep grass slope. My solution is to send the rest of the party down the gentle south ridge of Black Hill to Durisdeer, while I myself go down the ankle-tester slope for the car. The ** quality rating is for the lucky members of the party who go right through to Durisdeer.*

START/FINISH: Toll Cottage, at the foot of the road climb into the Dalveen Pass (GR 899068)

A gate at the roadside leads into the bottom of the cleuch. Head up the stream, keeping close to, or in, the water, for maximum entertainment value. At the 340m contour is a little grassy hollow, with two waterfalls dropping into it. Go up a slope of scree, grass and rock to left of the left-hand waterfall to a small tree. Traverse right, just below the tree, to the top of the waterfall - this is fairly exposed, but the tree is a reassuring handhold and the footholds are good.

Cross the stream at the waterfall top, and go straight up to the crest of the rocky rib beyond. This crest, of firm rock and grass, runs up into the steep grass slope above.

When the slope eases, contour across rough grass and cross the top of the stream on the right to a gate in the fence beyond. Head westwards up grassy slopes to the trig at the summit of Black Hill.

For those who do not need to return to the start-point, there is now the long gentle descent of the southward ridge, with two slight rises on the way down. At the foot of the ridge you look down onto the treetops and church tower of Durisdeer. Cross the stream on the left to a gate onto the Well Pass track at the edge of the village.

To return to the start-point, head northwest from Black Hill's summit. A knoll on the extreme corner of the plateau is called Pettylung and gives an intimidating view down onto the Dalveen road. Head down the steep spur to the road corner.

Walk 2:4
** WELL HILL and PASS, with PENBANE, BLACK HILL
5$^{1}/_{2}$ miles 2100ft (8$^{1}/_{2}$km 650m)
Grassy hilltops, with a steep descent, then track: moderate
** Shorter version ROMAN FORT and BLACK HILL follows

Durisdeer's sixteenth-century church has a Covenanting martyr in the graveyard, and a simple interior with panelled box pews. At the back is the tomb of the Dukes of Queensberry, which should certainly be visited before or after this walk.

The ornate marble tombstone is spectacularly out of place in this simple setting. It has everything: one imagines the sculptor Van Nost saying "Do you want marble cherubs?" "Oh yes." "And imitation velvet swags made of marble?" "Yes, we'll have some of those." "Barley-sugar columns?" "Them too." How was this all paid for? The 2nd Duke was the senior of the "Parcel of Rogues in a Nation" who negotiated the Treaty of Union with England in 1707; he was rewarded with a pension of £3000 a year.

Durisdeer is a place of literary pilgrimage for admirers of Salman

THE LOWTHER HILLS

Rushdie. The action of 'Satanic Verses' arrives most unexpectedly in Durisdeer. The various disguised archangels, Everest ascensionists etc take time off from the convoluted plot to climb a few tops around the village.

Well Hill, Penbane and Black Hill are presumably the tops concerned. They are not the highest: Well Hill doesn't quite achieve 2000ft (610m). They are, though, the nicest. Their steep sides look down folded stream valleys onto the Roman Road and the Dalveen Pass. Southwards the view is the length of Nithsdale to Criffel and the Solway. The grassy ridge for the ascent, and the grassy track to finish, alike provide easy access to the higher level. And Penbane has the nicest little summit in Galloway.

MAP: Landranger 78 (Nithsdale) or Harveys Lowther Hills

START/FINISH at Durisdeer

❈　❈　❈

Take the street to right of the church. After a gate at the end of the village it becomes track. After 50yds, take a metal gate on the left. Cross the stream to the foot of the long grassy ridge of Black Hill. Large earthworks decorate the base of the hill.

In the course of the ascent, you will notice the small Roman fort in the valley on the right. At Black Hill's trig point, turn east, on

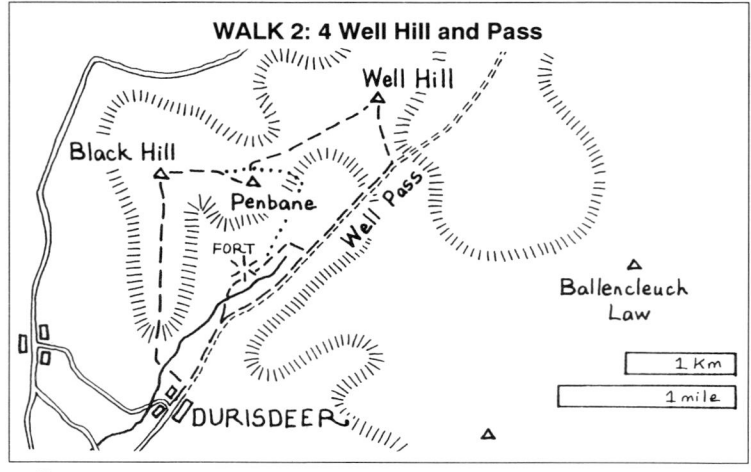

SOUTHERN LOWTHERS

grassy ground that is flat to start with, with the next objective, Penbane, temporarily concealed below the plateau. A fence joins from the left for the grassy descent to the col before Penbane. Go straight up this small pointed peak. (It can be omitted, simply dropping left to a gate in the fence.)

At Penbane's summit turn left, down steep grassy slopes, to a heathery col. A gate in the fence is down left. Turn back alongside the fence, then leave it to cross the grassy top unnamed on the Landranger map. Here is a quad bike path that formed during the rebuilding of the fence.

After the unnamed top, a short drop leads back to the fence. Follow it up to the summit of Well Hill.

Turn right, through a wooden gate, and go down alongside a fence with broken wall. The slope becomes steep, with rabbit-holes, short heather, and scree, to reach the track at the top of the Well Pass. Turn right, between fine stone gateposts. This is the old coach-road to Edinburgh: it runs down the left-hand side of the valley in a long gentle sweep. Mountain cyclists here are tempted to excess of speed: the cross-ditches have damaged both rider and machine.

On the other side of the valley is the line of the Roman Road, now invisible. Ahead, the coach road leads comfortably down to Durisdeer. However, 1/4 mile (1/2km) before the fort, the wall below the track has a wooden stile over it. If you wish to visit the fort, go down the heather to cross this stile. A track leads left, past the fort. After the fort the track fords the stream and rejoins the coach road.

** VARIANT: ROMAN FORT and BLACK HILL
3 miles 1200ft (5km 350m) moderate
Shorter than the main walk but otherwise just as good, this takes in the Roman fort and a charming little stream valley.

Take the street past the church to the gate at the end of the village, and the track (old coach road) beyond. The second gate on the left leads onto a muddy track that crosses the stream and climbs to the Roman fort. This small square structure finds a modern use as storage for black plastic bags of silage.

Continue along the track, which overlies the old Roman Road, then head around the base of the hill to the left, on boggy ground, to a sheep fank beside a small stream. A path above on the right

THE LOWTHER HILLS

follows the stream up into its hollow. The hollow is, briefly, steep-sided and slightly rocky.

At the col above, go round to left of the abundant heather. A small path runs along the base of Penbane. This path formed during the Karrimor Mountain Marathon of 1993 and has been kept open by sheep. From the col beyond Penbane, head up the steep grass of Black Hill, with a fence alongside on the right to start with. Flat ground above leads (in mist, it's west) to the trig point.

Turn south, to find the top of the long grassy ridge leading down towards Durisdeer. You go through two gates and up two slight rises on the way down. At the ridge foot turn left, to cross the stream. A metal gate leads back onto the coach road at the edge of the village.

Walk 2:5
* GLENIMP
7 miles 1700ft (11$^{1/2}$km 500m)
Short version 5 miles 1400ft (7$^{1/2}$km 400m)
An awkward stream valley, then grassy ridgetops and tracks: moderate/hard

It's not the tops of the Lowthers that matter, but the insides. This walk and the next crawl into the hidden stream valleys, and find small waterfalls and unexpected trees. Either of the walks will fit conveniently into that part of Sunday before the Durisdeer church tea.

MAP: Landranger 78 (Nithsdale) or Harveys Lowther Hills

EXTENSIONS: This walk can be combined in various ways with parts of the following one. The two are therefore presented on the same map. For a full day, combine the short version with Walk 2:4 (reversed), or the long version with Walk 2:7.

START/FINISH: Durisdeer (GR 895037)

❋ ❋ ❋

Take the road back out of the village for 200yds, and turn left before the cemetery onto a track. This ancient roadway runs towards the deep hill-slot of Glenaggart, which is the way we shall be coming down from this walk. After the first gate, and just as the track starts

SOUTHERN LOWTHERS

to climb, turn up left to pass through a gate to right of stone sheep-enclosures.

Drop gently left, on a grass path through bracken, to the Glenimp stream. The stream will be followed to its head. The only paths are made by sheep or goats: the valley is narrow, and steep-sided.

Cross the stream and go up a few feet to a small path along the valley wall. This crosses a rocky slope between scattered trees just above the stream, then drops back to the water. Go upstream, crossing frequently. After a mile (1½km) the stream forks. Take the left-hand valley, which has scattered trees and small waterfalls. It

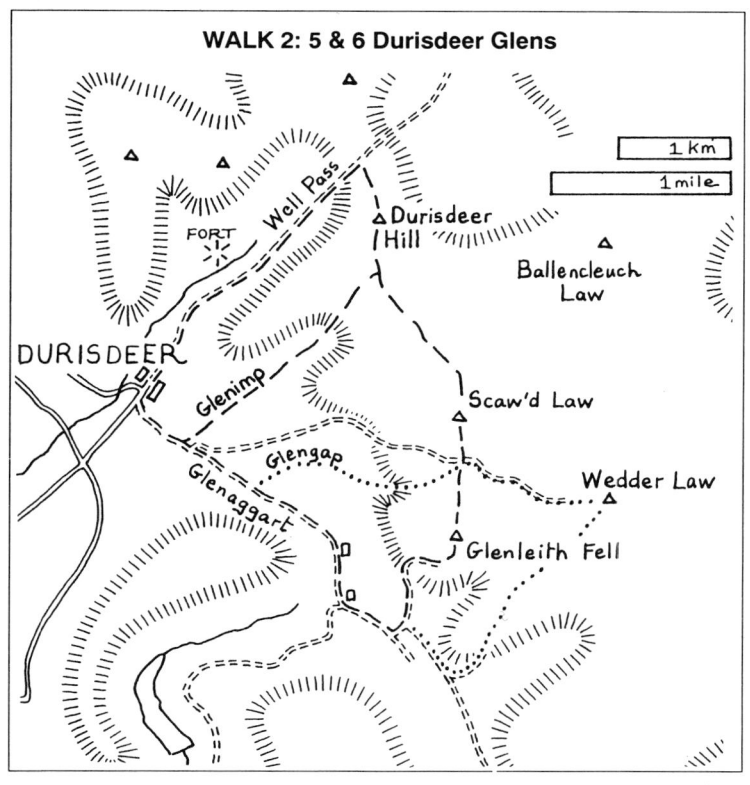

WALK 2: 5 & 6 Durisdeer Glens

THE LOWTHER HILLS

reaches the ridge-top at the col between Durisdeer Hill and Scaw'd Law, with a fence crossing in front.

SHORT VERSION: turn left, alongside the fence, which soon becomes a wall. It leads over Durisdeer Hill and down, fairly steeply, to the track at the head of the Well Pass. (Do not short-cut to left: slopes are steep and heathery.) Turn left down the clear grassy track to Durisdeer.

MAIN WALK: Turn right, and follow the fence, which soon becomes a wall, up to the summit of Scaw'd Law. Drop alongside the wall (this wall being to left), and bear off right along a fence to join a stony track at a gate. (GR 924032) **AT THIS POINT YOU COULD TRANSFER TO THE FINAL SECTION OF WALK 2:6, TO ADD 1$^{1}/_{2}$ MILES (2KM) TO THE WALK**.

Go through the gate, and turn back right along the fence's upper side. After a rough $^{3}/_{4}$ mile (1km) with bits of old fence wire among the heather, the fence starts to descend. Now the tiny cairn that marks the grassy summit of Glenleith Fell is 100yds away on the left.

Leave the summit southwards for 150yds, to find a faint track marked with a few fence-posts. Turn right, southwest. The track slants down the face of Glenleith Fell, becoming gradually clearer, and zigzagging as the slope steepens. It has a fine outlook over the lower hills around Kettleton to Nithsdale, and northwards to Lowther Hill; these views are particularly enjoyable after the cosy but enclosed ascent route.

The track reaches the flat ground of Blackhill Moss, where it is joined by two other tracks from the left, then bends right to pass the abandoned shepherd's house above the head of the Kettleton glen. The track passes a second abandoned house at the head of Glenaggart. It goes down easily inside the narrow valley to rejoin the outward route for the final mile back to Durisdeer.

SOUTHERN LOWTHERS

Walk 2:6
GLENGAP and WEDDER LAW
8 miles 1800ft (13km 550m)
Another awkward stream valley, then grassy ridgetops and tracks: moderate/hard
See combined map walks 2:5 & 2:6 (p51)

This walk is the twin of Walk 2:5: again it offers the ascent of a slightly rocky stream valley, followed by a short walk over the tops and an easy track descent. Parts of the two walks can be combined in various ways, so that you can decide whether you want a short walk, or a moderately long one, before your Durisdeer church tea. For easier planning, I have put the two walks onto a single map.

MAP: Landranger 78 (Nithsdale) or Harveys Lowther Hills

**EXTENSION: for a full day, combine this with Walk 2:7

START/FINISH: Durisdeer (GR 895037)

❈ ❈ ❈

Take the road back out of the village. Just before the cemetery, a track leads left towards the gap of Glenaggart. This goes through a gate at the foot of the first stream valley leading up left: that valley is Glenimp, the line of the previous walk. Here the track enters the bottom of Glenaggart, and after another 600yds ($^1/_2$km), it crosses a second stream before starting to climb. The valley of this stream is Glengap.

Go up alongside the stream, on a clear sheep path. Soon the steep-sided little valley forks. Follow the right-hand stream. The going is now steeper and more awkward. Very small crags are above the stream. One possibility here is a wet-foot route over the mossy rocks in the stream bed.

After a mile the valley ascends more gently, with more straightforward walking. Stay alongside the stream to its very top. Here you meet a fence on the right, and the Landrover track coming down from the left, with a gate where it passes through the fence. (GR 924032) **AT THIS POINT YOU COULD TRANSFER TO THE FINAL SECTION OF WALK 2:5, TO SHORTEN THE WALK BY $1^1/_2$ MILES (2KM).**

THE LOWTHER HILLS

Once through the gate the track dips into a col, and climbs most of the way up Wedder Law. The actual summit of this is on the wrong (left-hand) side of the fence: there is a gate just past the summit.

From the gate, a faint quad-bike track, marked by occasional posts, heads southwest down the long gentle spur of Tansley Rig. After 1$^{1/2}$ miles (2km) this drops left, to the top of a clearer track. This leads down to meet a horizontal track at the foot of the slope.

Turn right, and follow this new track as it crosses the Glenleith Burn and climbs slightly to a junction. Turn down left. The track soon bends back right, passing two abandoned shepherd's cottages and the head of the Kettleton Burn, where there is a nice view down to the reservoir (Walk 2:7). After passing a second cottage it drops into the narrow slot of Glenaggart. Descend the valley to rejoin the outward route.

Walk 2:7
** KETTLETON and CAMPLE
9$^{1/2}$ miles 1300ft (15km 400m)
Short section of rough moorland; narrow path across steep slope in Cample Cleuch; low grassy hills, path and track: mod/hard

---

While the main ridge of the Southern Lowthers is grass with fences, streams flowing into Nithsdale have carved the western slopes into the steep-sided stream valleys called 'cleuchs'. The most interesting ground is here. At 381m, East Morton Hill is roughly half the height of Queensberry, but could still be reckoned as the better hill. Kettleton harbours a little loch, and Cample Cleuch harbours wild goats.

MAP: Landranger 78 (Nithsdale) or Harveys Lowther Hills

START/FINISH: Grass verge at or near the bottom of the Burn farm track (GR 903982)

※　※　※

The tarred farm lane leads past Burn farm to the Water Board cottages at the Shaw. Go through the lower of two gates ahead, and take the track northwards through a small wood to the dam of the Kettleton Reservoir. The dam was built in the last century by men

SOUTHERN LOWTHERS

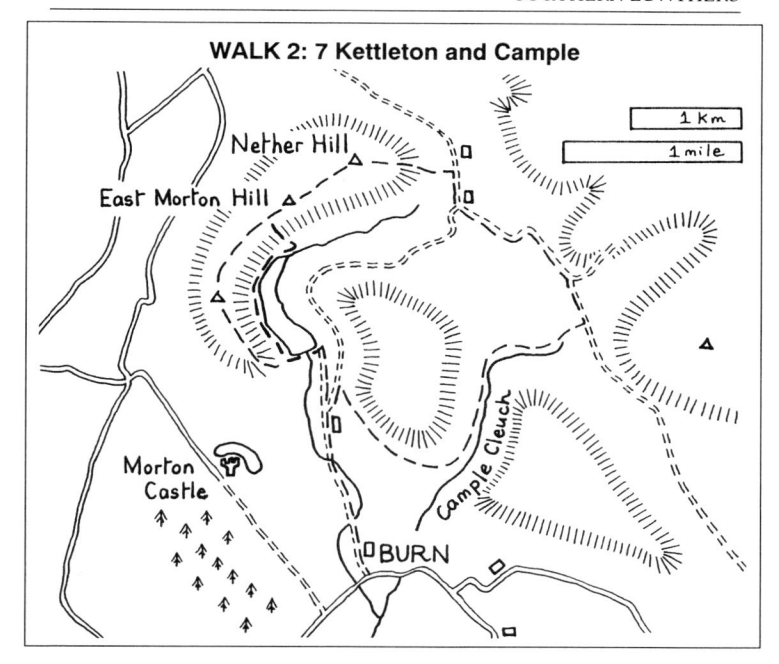

with wheelbarrows, and the paths they made to dig building-stone can be seen on the hillside across the stream. Given a hundred years to settle in, the reservoir has blended into its surroundings; it helps that it is almost always full, so shows no scarred shoreline.

At the dam end is a hard standing used by fishers who've driven up the rough track.

Cross the dam to a stile. Here one could continue up the steep slope ahead onto the hill with the ancient settlement, but lakeside walks are so rare hereabouts that we prefer to turn north along the reservoir side. A small path above the fence leads along the foot of the steep slope of the Settlement Hill. After the tumbledown boathouse, the path becomes a mere sheep trod alongside the fence.

At the head of the reservoir, the way may be obstructed by bracken in July and August. Here a stream runs down the slope of East Morton Hill on the left. Turn up this stream's small slot. This

THE LOWTHER HILLS

Northern Lowthers seen from Kettleton Loch

cuts back into the slope, giving a sheltered and less steep ascent. At the top, turn right up grassy slopes. East Morton's summit is a tuft of rushes.

The steepness of the slope conceals the col leading onwards towards Nether Hill. The col is due east, further right than you'd expect, and lies below a dark heathery knoll on the opposite slope. Go through the gate in the col and ascend over, or to left of, the heathery knoll. Now the ridge turns north (left), to circle the head of another deepcut stream. Wheelmarks of quad bikes make an easy path.

It's hard to say where may be the top of Nether Hill - the Ordnance Survey thinks it's the northwestern knoll, Harveys disagrees. But surely it's beneath us to go bagging a 393m peak, and better is to circle the left-hand, northern edge. This gives a view down into the cleuch of Glenaggart to Durisdeer. Descend off the plateau eastwards, down a short steep slope. At the top of the pass stand a ruined house and a shelter shed, but these are hidden under the curve of the slope. The parish boundary fence descending the opposite slope gives the point to aim for.

At the bottom of the slope turn right, above a fence, to a gate. This opens onto the track through the Glenaggart pass.

Turn right along the track. You look down into the deep Kettleton valley, and reach another ruined house. (Here a branch-track on the right gives a short return to the walk's start-point.) After another 600yds ($^1/_2$km) the track turns left, uphill. Ignore the branch-track on the right, and continue up the main track for another 200yds, before turning off right. The new track drops to cross the Glenleith Burn near a metal shed, and then, after another $^1/_2$ mile ($^3/_4$km) reaches the Berry Grain at a stream junction.

Turn off down the right bank of the Berry Grain, staying beside the water as it enters its deep valley to reach the junction with the Glenleith Burn. These two streams have carved out between them a deep secluded hollow in the hill. Here you are likely to meet the Lowther herd of wild goats. Particularly impressive are the high-leaping, high-scented, highly hairy billies. They're unafraid, and let you get just not quite close enough for a decent photo. Trick them by taking a telephoto lens...

Cross the Glenleith Burn to go down along the right bank of the

THE LOWTHER HILLS

combined stream, which is now the Cample. After 50yds, the way is blocked by a scree scaur. Do not take the rising path, but drop to the stream and make a way along the foot of the scaur. Continue along the narrow bank for 300yds. Now the bank ahead drops steeply into the stream, but you can make your way up the slope on the right to a path that contours along above.

This path is very narrow, and though the drop to the stream is only some 50ft (20m), it feels quite exciting. It passes above some small waterfall pools, to reach a large cairn. The path rounds a final corner, and the little triangular landscape you've been seeing at the end of the slot widens to become Nithsdale. The path rises to join a track above. The track, long-abandoned, was originally used to gather stone for field walls. It leads to a gate at the top of the enclosed ground.

Do not go through this gate, but turn right along the field wall. The path, just above the wall, is a sheep one, not a people one, and in high summer you may have to push through some more bracken. After $^{3}/_{4}$ mile (1km), the wall drops to meet a track. Turn left, down the track, to come down through the upper of the two gates at the Water Board cottages.

Walk 2:8
* QUEENSBERRY from MITCHELLSLACKS
$7^{1}/_{2}$ miles 2000ft (12km 600m)
Track and grassy hill, moderate
* Extension over EARNCRAIG HILL
$8^{1}/_{2}$ miles 2500ft (14km 750m): moderate/hard
* Extension over EARNCRAIG and GANA HILLS
11 miles 2900ft (18km 900m): moderate

Queensberry is the highest, and also the most southerly, of the Southern Lowthers. Accordingly it stands out from the range, dominating lower Nithsdale and looking deep into England. It is the point from which you can see into every section of this book, if not perhaps every individual walk. Its windswept heights are complemented by a return along the enclosed little glen of the Capel Burn (but not on the 11-mile version: that one returns along the enclosed little glen of the Garroch Water).

Depending on how lucky you are with the sheep trods, the lower slope of Wee Queensberry is tussocky, and so is the col between it and

SOUTHERN LOWTHERS

the main hill. However, the descent is on comfortable grass, and a rough track is ready to convey you back to your car.

Earncraig Hill is distinguished as the lowest 2000-footer hill in the Southern Uplands: distinguished also by some definite rocky bits, and should certainly be included if the legs of the party are up to the rougher ground and the extra mile. If the legs are up to three extra miles and you're enjoying the hills, the final variant over Gana Hill grabs an extra one.

MAP: Landranger 78 (Nithsdale) or Harveys Lowther Hills

START/FINISH: roadside above the track to Mitchellslacks (GR 965960)

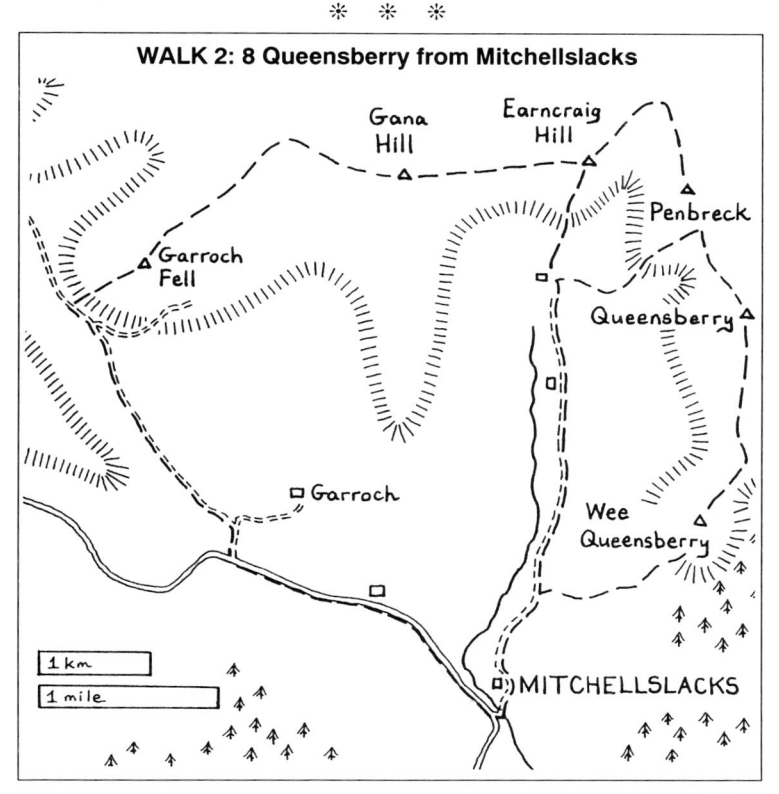

❋   ❋   ❋

WALK 2: 8 Queensberry from Mitchellslacks

THE LOWTHER HILLS

Take the farm track across the Capel Water, and left, past the farm. It leads through two gates and up into the valley of the Capel Burn. After a mile (1½km), just before the prominent hummock of the Law, a track branches right, and descends to sheep enclosures. Go through a gate, and round to left of the pens, then behind them to cross a stream. A grassy, and somewhat tussocky, ridge leads up onto Wee Queensberry. The going becomes easier; the flat ridge above and the final cone are pleasant walking.

Descend northwards, with trees below on the right, to cross a boggy col, and go up the slope of Queensberry: again, going becomes easier once above the col. Small boulder fields and rocky outcrops are passed, or crossed, and there are two upstanding cairns.

The hills here are well supplied with such cairns. Old photographs show them to go back into the last century (ie. the nineteenth), and their purpose is a mystery to the present-day farmers. Two theories suggest themselves. They may be placed to indicate the break of the slope - a shepherd passing the cairn will be able to see both the gentle slope above and the steeper slope below. I prefer the "five o clock" theory. A shepherd returning to the farmyard at 4:30 will be found one more task to complete the day, and that task may keep him busy till six. A shepherd returning at five will be allowed home. Therefore, a shepherd will wish to find himself some task to occupy that strategic half-hour up on the hill.

Some cairns do have a more recent history. The one at GR 960965 was built by idle extras during the filming of *Thirty-nine Steps*. The one at GR 988989, which the route now passes, was identified on the map and chosen for a control point on the 1994 Karrimor Mountain Marathon. The controllers then discovered that it didn't actually exist, and were obliged to build it.

From Queensberry's first summit cairn, a flat plateau leads northeast to the large, ancient one.

Descend a broad grassy spur northwards: in mist a compass-bearing will be required, until a fence joins from the right. The col before Penbreck has peat-hags: in clear weather pass round these to the left; in mist stay along the fence as the hags aren't too bad. Follow the fence onto the first, southeastern knoll of Penbreck. The main route now descends left. (The longer routes, described below,

SOUTHERN LOWTHERS

continue along the fence.)

Go down the grassy spur into a steep-sided stream hollow. Follow the stream down to the bothy at Burleywhag. This small shelter, maintained by the Mountain Bothies Association, is usually welcoming with its small stove, though very occasional anti-social users leave it in states varying from unpleasant to intolerable.

Cross the wooden bridge, and take a faint and boggy track down-valley. It rises to join the fence above, and after a rail-gate becomes clear and distinct. It passes below a small wooded stream gorge, and then traverses the steep valley side on the flank of the Law: a diversion can be made to include this attractive knoll on the left. The outward route is rejoined for the final mile past the farm.

* EXTENDED ROUTE over EARNCRAIG HILL
8½ miles 2500ft (14km 750m): moderate/hard

Having crossed Queensberry as on the previous route, follow the fence over the grassy hill of Penbreck (Gaelic Beinn Bhreac, Speckled Hill). Stay alongside the fence, northwards: it is tempting to drop into the stream hollow on the left, but this descent is of broken ground with scree. Stay with the fence, then, down fairly steep grass, and then left to cross the head of the steep-sided little valley. Go up the grassy slopes, steeply and then more gently, to the summit of Earncraig Hill. The corner of a stone wall provides sandwich-eating shelter.

Descend the rough slope southwards, with no path. There are one or two small crags, so a little care is needed. The slope becomes uncomfortably heathery for its final descent to the bothy, where the shorter route is rejoined.

* FURTHER EXTENDED ROUTE over EARNCRAIG and GANA HILLS
11 miles 2900ft (18km 900m): moderate

Having crossed Queensberry as on the previous route, follow the fence northwards over the grassy hill of Penbreck and into the hollow beyond. The fence continues sharply back left to the summit of Earncraig.

Now with wall alongside, the fence continues to guide down a steep grass slope and across a wide col. Where it turns right, keep

THE LOWTHER HILLS

Leaving the summit of Queensberry

ahead over a plateau of knolls, westward, and rejoin the fence in the col beyond. The fence, with a small path some yards to its left, leads on over the summit of Gana Hill.

Continue westwards with the fence, descending then level, for ³/₄ mile (1km). The fence has a railed gate, and this gate is the best point to slant away left on the long flat ridge to Garroch Fell. (Turning away earlier will lead to peat-hags.) A fair-sized cairn decorates the end-point of the ridge.

From the cairn, you can drop off, or roll off, or otherwise struggle down deep heather westwards to the track below: or else walk down south to find a faint track slanting down right, to reach the same track below. To left, the bottom track descends into the green valley of the Garroch Water, which it fords some six or seven times before emerging at some sheep-handling pens and sheds.

Turn right past the sheds onto the rough track of Garroch farm, to reach the hill road. Two miles (3km) along the verge returns you to the start-point.

Walk 2:9

QUEENSBERRY from the EAST

$8^{1/2}$ miles 1800ft ($13^{1/2}$km 550m)

Grassy slopes: moderate

*To the east of the Daer Reservoir lies a range of small hills covered in large trees. This makes any approach to the Lowthers from this direction fairly unrewarding. At the southern end, though, a hill road runs in to Kinnelhead, and open slopes lead onto Queensberry itself. Craighoar Hill and Harestanes are slightly rocky on top, so that this walk is not just a resource for those stuck on the wrong side of the Lowthers, but almost gets a star * for quality.*

MAP: Landranger 78 (Nithsdale)

From Beattock a small road leads westwards into the hills: it's the beginning of a less exciting stretch of the Southern Upland Way through all those trees. Follow it for $3^{1/2}$ miles ($5^{1/2}$km) to its end at Kinnelhead. Parking space just before the bridge over the Kinnel Water.

START/FINISH: Kinnelhead (GR 033016)

⁂ ⁂ ⁂

Ahead, a stern sign says "Kinnelhead: Private Road", a light-hearted one "Please Drive Slowly Through the Town". Follow the tarred farm track through Kinnelhead farm and on to Blairmack. On the left, the craggy end of Craighoar looms above a patch of forest.

Cross the burn at Blairmack and continue through two gates on a rough track. After 500yds at an X-junction keep ahead, and after another 100yds, turn off the track to go straight uphill beside the edge of the plantation on the left. The climb is a comfortable one on short grass and moss.

At the top of the trees, slant left up to the small cairn at the top of Craighoar. It's a fine viewpoint, with a sharp drop at your feet to the Threepen Burn. Continue westwards over grass with plenty of rocks sticking out and occasional small pools. Each rocky knoll has its own cairn. Were these cairns recent, one might be tempted to dismantle them, but they are historic and built by shepherds, and in this bleak upland may be valued for their decorative effect. In navigational terms they are of no help, tending rather to confuse; this may be considered a further point in their favour.

WALK 2: 9 Queensberry from the East

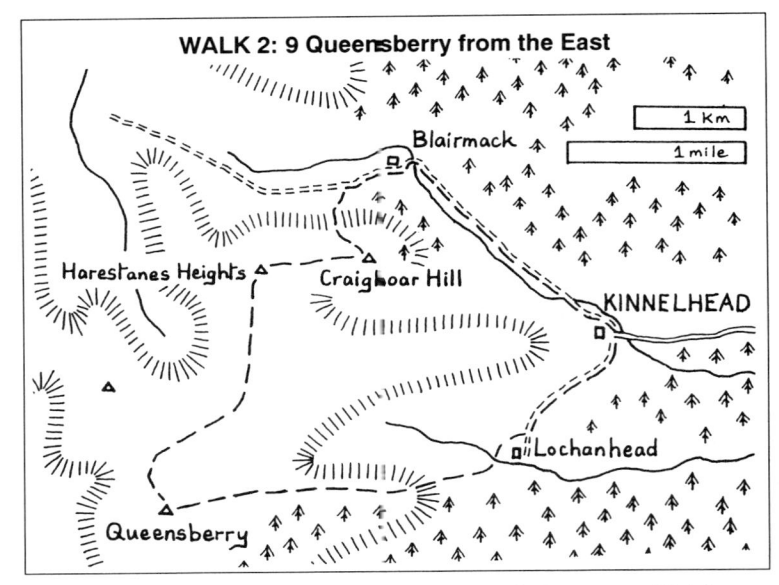

After the first and higher (578m) top of Harestanes Heights, continue southwards over ground that remains quite rocky. The stone wall through the col can be crossed, with care, at the highest point, where a small post assists. The cairn on the southern top widens half-way up, and from afar looks like a stout hillwalker. From this cairn, aim directly for the summit of Queensberry on 230° magnetic: this bearing passes to left of the peat-hags in the col, and then skirts the western slopes of Mount Glass. An 80m climb leads to the regional boundary fence. Cross it, and climb a further 100m to Queensberry's summit. A fine view southwards over the Solway Firth to the hills of England awaits you at the ancient cairn.

Descend northeast to a gate at the highest point of the regional boundary fence (GR 992001), and go down the broad, ill-defined spur, then across right, to the edge of the forest. The descent is gentle and squelchy. Forget about dry feet and enjoy the rapid downhill progress. 200yds above Lochanhead the Lochan Burn joins from the left. Cross it, and work round above the stone wall to join the Lochanhead access track. This track leads northeast for a mile (1½km) to join the Kinnelhead track just west of the walk's start.

Black Hill and Durisdeer (Walk 2:4) from East Morton Hill (Walk 2:7)
In the Penbreck Gap (Walk 2:8)

Tynron Doon and Auchengibbert (Walk 3:1) seen across wooded Nithsdale

Morton Castle and Loch (Walk 3:4)

Criffel blocks off the end of Nithsdale, from Settlement Hill

3: Nithsdale

Nithsdale is one of the gaps where the ice came through from the north. Now it's a wide valley of fields and woodlands, with a famous salmon river and a pink castle. Behind the fields, the gentle slopes of the Lowther and Carsphairn hills form a bumpy background.

If Nithsdale is one of the more attractive of these former ice-highways, it's because of that castle - for the influence of the Dukes of Buccleuch has reached out further than the pink walls and parkland of Drumlanrig. Nithscale does have some ugly spruce plantations, but they are tucked away in odd corners, such as the Euchan Glen, not visible from the castle windows. Patches of ancient woodland have been preserved, and new ones have been planted piecewise, to make a mixed landscape of field and forest.

Here are gentle walks in the woods, for days when the hilltops are clouded and chilly. One is at the castle itself, while another, further east, offers a small but spectacular gorge where the waterfalls will be at their best during a long wet season.

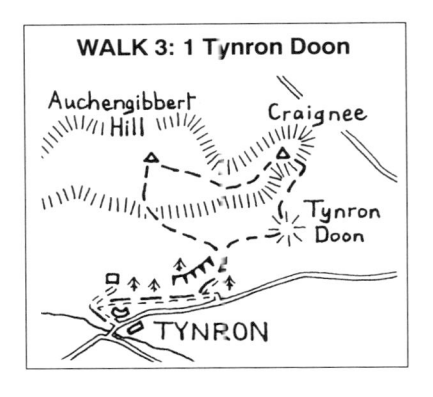

Walk 3:1
* TYNRON DOON
4 miles 1000ft (6$^{1/2}$km 300m)
Smooth but steep grassy hillsides: easy/moderate

The steep-sided, flat-topped hill fort of Tynron Doon stands as a watchtower above the village of Penpont. Its final section is splendidly steep, and its flat top just asks for a picnic to be spread. While the grown-ups are enjoying the strawberries, the well-shaken champagne and the intimate views onto Nithsdale, the children will be having fun in the grass ditches that encircle the plateau at various levels.

The extra hill, Auchengibbert, offers wider views, extending across several ranges to Curlywee and Lamachan in the west. The ridge joining the two tops is short and walkable grass. However, lower slopes are trampled by cows, and can be muddy: wellingtons are suitable footwear.

MAP: Landranger 78 (Nithsdale)

START/FINISH: Tynron village (GR 806930)

✳   ✳   ✳

Start at the centre of Tynron village, and take the lane beside the bridge. This soon becomes a rough track, and rises through a wood to a junction. Turn sharp right, onto the lower of two tracks.

This new track descends a little, and gives a view back down onto the chimney pots of Tynron. After ³/₄ mile (1km) it passes below a quarry, and here a muddy branch track runs steeply uphill. It leaves the trees at a gate, and here turn left, uphill, along the edge of the plantation and through a second gate. Tynron Doon is over on the right, and the returning route will come back through this same gate.

Muddy tractor wheelmarks run on uphill, with a parallel wall on the right, to a gate at the top left corner of the field. Slant up left, northwest, across damp grass slopes to the trig point at the summit of Auchengibbert Hill.

From Auchengibbert Hill head back east along the grassy ridge. After 100yds, you drop into an unexpected dip with a boggy bottom where you cross a broken wall. After ¹/₂ mile (800m) a subsidiary top is reached. Tynron Doon is visible below, but to gain an extra top

THE LOWTHER HILLS

and to avoid a steep descent, head left along the continuing ridge to the outlier of Craignee.

The descent of Craignee's southeastern flank is briefly quite steep, with very small rocky outcrops. After dropping about 50ft (15m vertical), contour out right: a grassy path forms above the line of a fence, and leads into the col before Tynron Doon. This col shows the furrows of an ancient field system. By working round to the right, to the line of the original entrance, you can avoid climbing in and out of the three contouring ditches that defend the summit of Tynron Doon.

Return to the col, and contour left, on a muddy path more used by sheep than people. The path descends towards the cragged outlump of Craigturra, aiming for the nearest corner of the forest that clothes it. Here the track of the outward route is rejoined.

Walk 3:2
DRUMLANRIG CASTLE and RIVER NITH
12 miles 900ft (19km 300m)
Tracks, paths, 1 mile (1½km) of road: easy

A full 5 miles (8km) of wooded riverbank is enough to excuse the necessary mile of road that links up the top end of the walk. It finishes with a ramble through the woods around the castle. Here you can ignore the described route and simply get lost among the trees - or you can carefully follow the indicated line, and still get lost... it doesn't matter, as downhill will lead to one of two tarred roads back to the castle.

MAP: Landranger 78 (Nithsdale) or, better, Harveys Lowther Hills

START/FINISH: car park at Drumlanrig Castle (GR 852994)

❊ ❊ ❊

Walk north along the castle's driveway, which bends round to the right through parkland. After 400yds of downhill, a sign points back left, "Riverside Walk".

The path leads through a narrow white gate (not the vehicle gate alongside) into the woods above the river. The path is carved in places out of the rocky bank, and runs down to a high metal footbridge. This bridge is falling to bits, and has been wrapped in

NITHSDALE

barbed wire to prevent your getting onto it. Turn back for a few steps, and take an uphill branch path to reach the track above.

Turn right along the track and follow it upstream. It is broad, flat, dry and covered in larch needles. However, after timber operations it can be muddy and rutted. The river below is a sequence of deep pools below banks of rock and earth. The valley narrows: as well as our ancient track and the river itself, the A76 and the railway have to be crammed in. The A76 came last and there wasn't really room: its northbound lane occasionally crumbles into the green waters below.

A mile (1½km) after the dangerous footbridge, the track divides. The lower branch is grassier. The tracks rejoin after another ½ mile (¾km). Opposite Enterkinfoot, take the track passing above a riverside house. This soon divides: stay on the upper branch. A wooden gate leads out into open fields where the track continues as grassed-over wheelruts. It runs above the scattered alder thickets of the river bank.

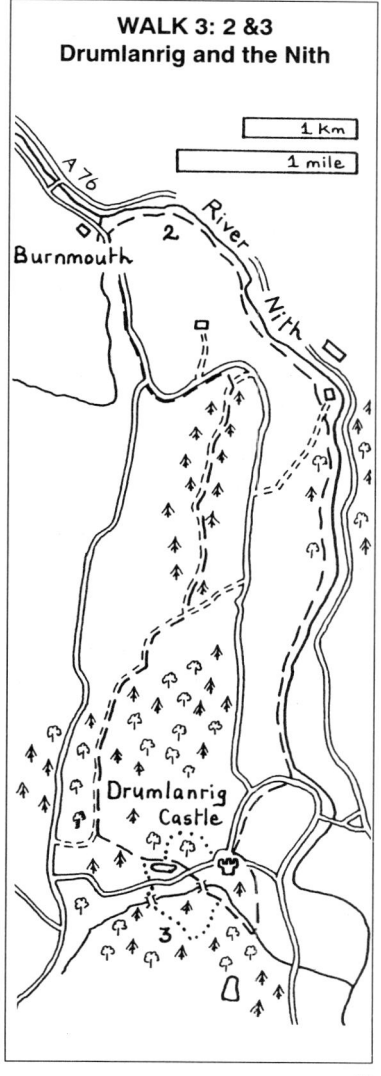

WALK 3: 2 &3
Drumlanrig and the Nith

After a mile (1¹/₂km) of field, it starts to slant up left away from the river, and emerges onto a minor road just north of Burnmouth farm.

Follow the road left, up the Burnsands Burn, to a junction just before three houses. Turn off left, uphill. This road could be followed back to Drumlanrig: it has little traffic, and views across to the Lowthers. However, our walk uses it for just 500yds (¹/₂km) of steep uphill. Just past the track end of Crairiepark farm, a wood on the right runs down to the road. Go through a gateless gateway to take a faint track uphill for 50yds, then turning left to contour through the woods above the road. The forgotten track is overhung by branches and soft with the leaf-fall of many winters. After 300yds it runs out into a well-used gravel road.

Turn right, uphill. The track zigzags, and at the beginning of what should be a long gentle downhill run, it has been resurfaced with small rocks. This will improve with time, pine-needles, mud and possibly an additional layer of even smaller rocks. The boulderfield ends after a mile - meanwhile you can enjoy green Nithsdale and the Lowthers, seen between the branches.

Two miles (3km) after leaving the road, bear right on a diagonal cross-track. This rises slightly to a small ruin (GR 844014), and bears left between fields. Re-enter woods, crossing two junctions. Ahead, the main track passes out into an open field (GR 840002).

At this point, the more adventurous can turn left on any path. The track running towards the castle from the west (101m spotheight near Holm of Drumlanrig) is a tarred one with speed bumps. If you reach this, turn left (east) for the castle: alternatively, if you reach the unbumped public road, turn right (south).

Meanwhile, the main route stays on the track as it crosses the open field and re-enters the woods to a cross-track. Turn left for a few steps, and take the upper of two paths slanting down to the right. This reaches the tarred track with the speed-bumps. Just to left is Druid's Loch, and a wheelchair-quality path branches left to pass round this.

At the foot of the small loch, turn right (away from the castle!) on the tarred track, and immediately left onto a track that crosses the Marr Burn on a stone bridge. A red-topped waymark indicates the path to left along the stream's far bank. After ³/₄ mile (1km), this reaches a footbridge at the back of the adventure playground. Pass

Drumlanrig Castle and its 300-year old sycamore

round right into open parkland, and follow its edge, left, past the entrance to the adventure playground, to the castle.

Walk 3:3
* DRUMLANRIG WOODLAND WALKS
Up to 3 miles 600ft (4^1/$_2$km 200m)
Waymarked paths: easy (see map p69)

START/FINISH: car park at Drumlanrig Castle (GR 852994)

❊ ❊ ❊

Drumlanrig Castle offers a variety of waymarked trails through the woods. The longest is the Yellow Trail. It's an enjoyable ramble through mixed woodland with small bodies of water, red squirrels and occasional glimpses out to the Lowther Hills and the pink sandstone castle. The paths and tracks can be a little muddy.

The castle also has a cafe, an adventure playground with two death-slides, and a selection of art treasures.

THE LOWTHER HILLS

Walk 3:4
MORTON CASTLE and LOCHS
2¼ miles (3½km)
Forest tracks: easy

Morton Castle is an ancient keep, recently rebuilt into a state of less dangerous ruination. It stands in a fine position under the Lowthers and above a small loch. During a recent winter there suddenly arrived in Morton Wood a second loch. It was this second stretch of water that persuaded me to disrupt the numbering of this section at the last minute, and include this very short walk on forest tracks.

MAP: Landranger 78 (Nithsdale) or Harveys Lowther Hills
START/FINISH: track side above Morton Loch (GR 889991)

❊   ❊   ❊

Go through the gate to visit Morton Castle, and then return to take the forest track opposite. There are occasional red-arrow waymarks. After ½ mile (¾km) the track enters a clearing, with views across Nithsdale to Kier Hill and Thornhill. Here is a track T-junction, with the waymark pointing left: however, keep ahead, going downhill under beech trees to a lower track at the head of the new loch.

Here a waymark points left: this is, confusingly, a remnant of a previous route of the woodland walk. Follow this arrow along to left of the water, and at the loch's foot keep ahead for 50yds to the fence at the forest edge. This leads to the left, uphill. The ground underfoot is moss, beech leaves and remnants of fence wire.

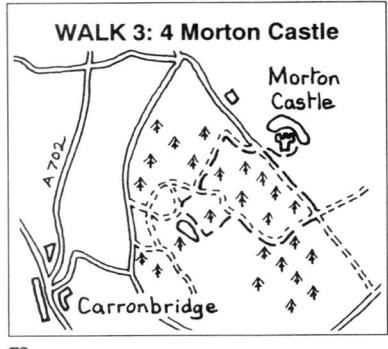

At the track above, the route rejoins the waymarked walk. Turn right along the track, with open ground on the right and Nithsdale views stretching from Criffel (ahead) by way of Tynron Doon to Cairnkinna (back right). Where the track forks, keep left. At the main, tarred track, turn left to reach Morton Castle after another ½ mile (¾km).

Walk 3:5
** CRICHOPE LINN
$2^{1}/_{2}$ miles 300ft (4km 100m)
Narrow path above cliffs: moderate

The small Linn Burn has carved itself a surprisingly deep gorge in the Nithsdale sandstone. This outstanding short walk peers into various hollows and caves. Be aware, though, that the path is narrow, and often muddy, and is alongside drops of 100ft (30m). Teenagers will be tempted to leap across the gorge, or to cross it on high fallen trees.

For the really adventurous, there's a possibility of traversing the stream bed all the way. In the lower gorge, this will require short sections of swimming. The upper gorge will require swimming, and also an abseil entry. The gorge offers various sporting abseils, though the rock is too soft and brittle for rockclimbing.

MAP: Landranger 78 (Nithsdale)

START/FINISH: Once you've left the A76 at Closeburn, brown signposts point towards the Linn. Car parking is in a small quarry at GR 955907

❊ ❊ ❊

Walk south, down the road, for 50yds. A brown signpost indicates the start of the path up the Linn.

The path enters gorse and divides. The main path is ahead: the right fork leads to the stream bank, where you can assess the stream crossing you'll need to use later if you return by the variant route on the south bank.

The path winds forward through deep woodland, with the stream on its right. A stile crosses a low fence, and now the first cliff rises on the left - the path runs along its overhanging foot. Here various mindless vandals have carved their autographs into the sandstone. Mr Clarke of Oswestry carved his in 1879.

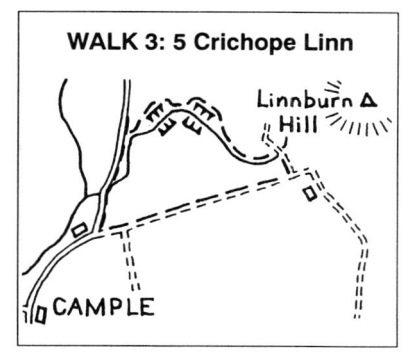

THE LOWTHER HILLS

Admire his stonecarving - mindless vandalism isn't what it used to be a century ago.

As the banks converge to form the lower gorge, a branch path runs across to a natural arch, through which you can admire a small waterfall. (The sandstone slabs here are damp and slippery.) The main path rises to the left, above the gorge. The gorge passed, it drops to rejoin the stream. Picnic tables on the opposite bank can be reached by leaping across the gorge, or, further upstream, by paddling. The main path stays on the north bank.

Above a second set of picnic tables on the opposite bank, the path rises to pass above the upper gorge. As it does so, it divides. The lower branch crosses a vertical earth bank high above the stream; the higher branch is less nerve-racking. At the top of this upper gorge the path drops towards the stream again. A side-path on the right lets you scramble down to examine the underground waterfall, where the stream drops into a deep slot.

After another 50yds the path divides again: the right fork crosses the stream to offer a possible return down the southern bank. (This short-cut return route is narrower and more exposed than the north bank has been.) The left fork continues up the north bank, and leads by a stile onto the Benthead farm track. Turn right on this track through a gate and across the stream, to turn right again on the Dollard track. This soon becomes a tarred lane that leads uphill at first, then descends with wide views of Nithsdale to a lower road. Turn right for $1/2$ mile ($3/4$km) to the start-point.

Walk 3:6
GLENKILN SCULPTURES with BENNAN
$6^{1}/_{2}$ miles 1000ft (10km 300m)
Track and road: rough heather on Bennan: moderate

This is a walk for special interest groups of two sorts. For lovers of modern sculpture there's a chance to see works by Epstein, Rodin and Moore standing around on sheep fields and stony hillsides. John the Baptist *looks down on early-morning fishermen; the two bits of Moore's* Reclining Figure *crouch beside a passing-place sign.*

The other interest group is the Marilyn-baggers. Marilyns are hills, however low, with 500ft (150m) of clear drop all round. Two of them can be snatched in a quick left and right from the head of the reservoir.

This walk aims to satisfy both groups. The 1300ft (398m) Bennan, with its curious summit structure, is combined with a visit to all of the sculptures. For those who prefer their art without hillwalking, four of the works are at the roadside, and the others a short walk away.

MAP: Landranger 84 (Dumfries)

EXTENSION: Bishop Forest Hill can also be ascended from *John the Baptist's* car park

START/FINISH: There's a small parking area at the head of the reservoir, under the pointing arm of John the Baptist (GR 839785)

Stroll up the road northwards for 400yds to visit Moore's *Standing Figure*. Return past the car park and along the reservoir side. The next sculpture, Moore's tall *Glenkiln Cross*, stands conspicuously, high above the road. Directly below the sculpture, look for a high grey field gate among trees. Go up a fairly steep grass slope to the sculpture.

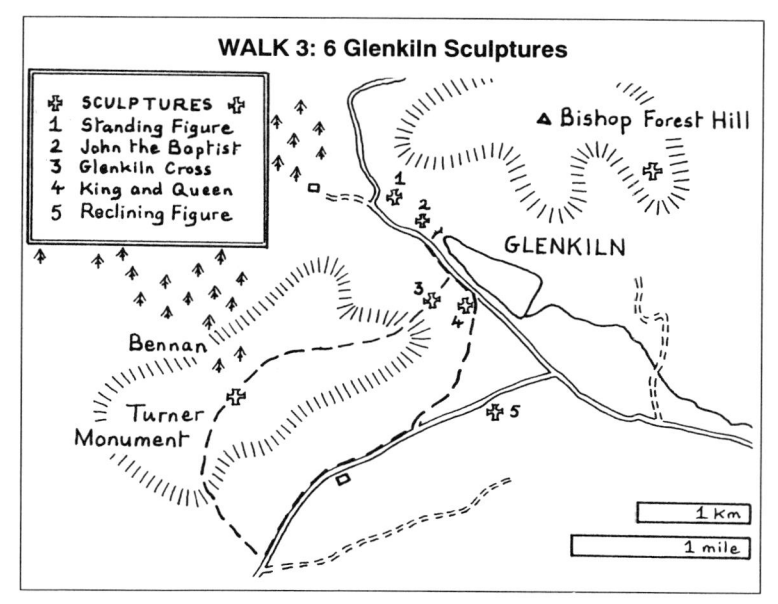

WALK 3: 6 Glenkiln Sculptures

SCULPTURES
1 Standing Figure
2 John the Baptist
3 Glenkiln Cross
4 King and Queen
5 Reclining Figure

THE LOWTHER HILLS

Moore's Reclining Figure No:1

Continue uphill to the 280m contour, where the slope eases. A fence crosses, with a gate of wooden rails 50yds away on the right. Go on up the gentle, rounded ridge, with a stone wall nearby on the left. 50yds to right of the wall are wheelmarks of a quad bike. These give easy passage through the wet heather to a gap in the wall at the 398m summit.

On that summit stands *Turner's Monument*. It has no great sculptural qualities but is an interesting ornamental feature, and adds more than the 2m needed to top the slightly exciting 400m contour. There's a view of three hill groups, from Queensberry to Cairnsmore, and across the Solway to England. A vague shadow in the south-west could easily be the Isle of Man.

Descend southwards over rough heather to a fence gate at GR 824763, then tend right to join a Landrover track that runs out onto the hill road beside a small pool. Turn left down the unfrequented road for 1¹/₂ miles (2km). Moore's *Reclining Figure No 1* is unmissable at the roadside on the right.

Return up the road for ¹/₂ mile (³/₄ km), until a track turns sharply back right. This passes below a plantation and contours round to pass just below the plinth of Moore's *King and Queen*, although at the time of writing, this sculpture is absent. Pass through a black iron gate to rejoin the road at the reservoir side, a ½ mile short of the car park.

The Sculptures

Rodin's *John the Baptist* and Moore's *Standing Figure* make a striking contrast, especially if you consider that they were made a mere half-century apart. *John* with his nicely-muscled bronze legs stands in a tradition going back to Michelangelo and the ancient Greeks. Moore's figure has holes in, and looks to have been assembled from various shapes out of the kitchen drawer.

That may be considered a slightly light-hearted sculpture, but the *Glenkiln Cross* is undeniably impressive, an ancient standing stone but with a human figure somehow occupying the same space.

The *Turner Monument* is a stone triangle 4m high, clearly visible from the main A75 road to the south. It was erected and inscribed by John Turner of Glen farm, and his bones now lie beneath it. But how did he know, as he carved the inscription, that he was doing so "four years before his death"?

Moore's *Reclining Figure No 1*, at the roadside, has (or have - there are two) been replaced by a glassfibre replica. Too many people were writing their names on them. Sadly, the *King and Queen*, who sat looking out over the reservoir, have also had to be removed; they were attacked by a vandal with a chainsaw in 1995. A replica will eventually be placed on the empty plinth.

Epstein's *Visitation* isn't marked on the map, so I have not given its location here. If you trace the walk described, you will notice it in a clump of Scots pines. It is said to portray the pregnant Mother of Christ. The actual model was a survivor of the concentration camps. It is a superb and moving work, enhanced by its rather bleak setting.

4: Carsphairn Hills

Until fairly recently, this out-of-the-way group of rounded grassy hills didn't even have a consistent name. They were the Cumnock Hills, or the Scaur Valley Hills, or the hills of Deugh, depending on where you were looking at them from. It was only with the publication in 1935 of Donald's Table of 2000ft tops that the group became the Carsphairn Hills, after its highest summit.

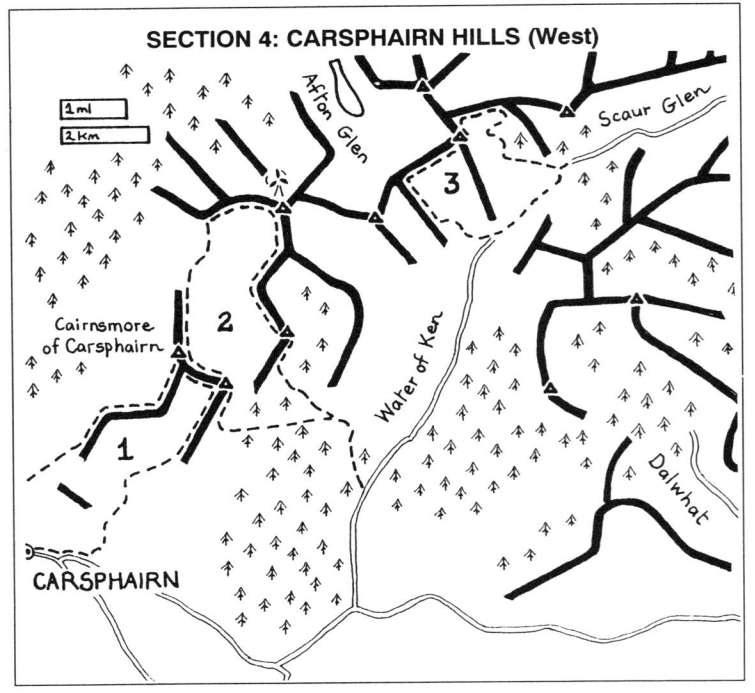

When a hill group is praised for its quality of solitude, one suspects that the reason people don't go there may be that it isn't worth going to. The Carsphairns are grassy-topped and boggy-bottomed, with fences running over. They are frequented by sheep, and by those who like to walk alone.

How important is such empty open space? Already, the valleys of the Carsphairns have been found convenient by the noisier sorts of industry. Any loud bangs you hear are from Dunside by the Kello Water, where metals that can't be welded in the normal way are blown together with dynamite. In the Euchan glen the Brocks fireworks factory used to test its imitation artillery, smoke-screen and shellfire. Most impressive was their low-technology harmless atomic bomb. Military jets practise low-flying in all Britain's mountains, but here they are allowed even lower (down to 100ft/30m).

Spreading green patches on the map show that most of the valleys and lower slopes are used for the industrial production of paper and low-grade building timber. Spruce plantations render the edges of the area unwalkable, even as their gravel roads are eroding away the remoteness of the inner hills. Of the dozen Scottish hills with Landrover tracks to their summits, four are in this guidebook: Wether Hill, Lowther and Green Lowther, and Windy Standard.

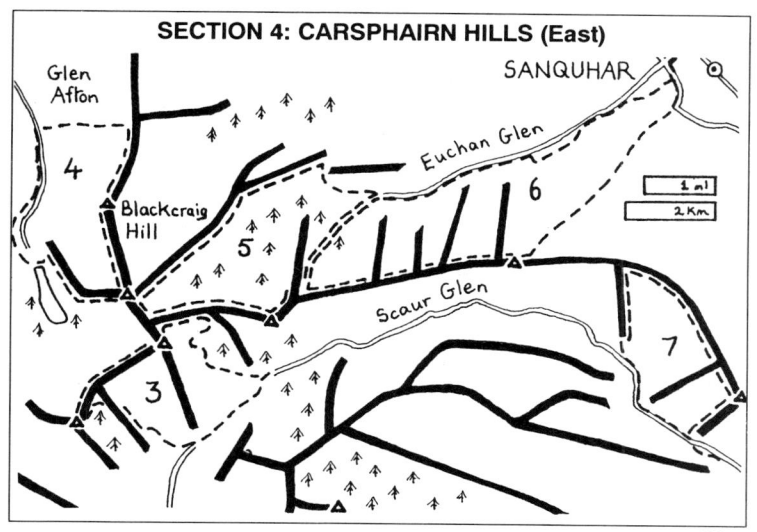

Merrick from Cairnsmore of Carsphairn

The track onto the plateau of Moorbrock Hill was built during mineral explorations - according to the planning agreement, it was to be removed when the explorations were done. The track onto Windy Standard serves the new wind farm.

The summit of Windy Standard is the place to stand and consider whether empty open space is valuable for its own sake. Wind power may turn out to be important in deferring the problems of global warming. Are the unfrequented, undeveloped and unexciting Carsphairn hills also important? Some people find the wind turbines rather handsome...

Still, there are other reasons, apart from political introspection, for visiting the Carsphairns. Those reasons are Blackcraig, and Cairnsmore of Carsphairn itself. These two rugged summits, one at either end of the range, raise their rocks above the tips of Windy Standard's turbine blades. Here are two patches of true mountain ground. And while six of the long quiet valleys have gone under the Christmas trees, lower Scaur and sweet Afton survive with their crags, their oaks, and their little silver rivers.

CARSPHAIRN HILLS

Walk 4:1
* CAIRNSMORE OF CARSPHAIRN from CARSPHAIRN
10 miles 2500ft (16km 750m)
Grassy going: moderate

Cairnsmore of Carsphairn is the highest hill in this book. It is one of Southern Scotland's seven Corbetts (hills over 2500ft), and it is the highest granite hill outside the Highlands. On all these counts it deserves respect, and should certainly be ascended. This route is the most convenient way to do so.

However, this is the grassy side of the mountain. For the brief mile from Beninner to the summit, we experience the rugged delights of Cairnsmore's eastern flank. A better route, for those with the time and the energy, is one that gets to grips with that rugged and rewarding side of it all (ie. Walk 4:2).

This route, though less good, is by no means bad. It has some bog on the way up, but a fine grassy ridge for the descent, and enjoyable views to Galloway and the Glenkens. It's an excellent second-best.

Carsphairn is a frontier village, on the borders of Galloway and Ayrshire, and with the slight air of desolation, even of desperation, that one associates with the frontier. However, it has a small and interesting museum (sorry, Heritage Centre) with a display of local pebbles arranged geologically. It also has an unexpected and welcome cafe and bar. Currently it is also permissible to park at Knockgray farm. The first one down to Carsphairn goes back up for the vehicle, the rest straight into the bar.

MAP: Landranger 77 (Dalmellington) or Outdoor Leisure 32 (Galloway)

START/FINISH: Carsphairn village (GR 562932) or Knockgray farm (GR 577933)

※　※　※

Head east along the main road, then bear left onto the B729 (Moniaive). After ¹/₄ mile (¹/₂km) turn up left onto the track for Knockgray farm. Just before the farm, a track leads left, uphill. Follow it up, past a plantation. At the 270m contour the track bends left: now follow the fence on the right as it continues uphill through a fairly wet area with rushes, to join a wall on the flank of Quantans Hill.

In the col beyond this flat summit things get even boggier. The

WALK 4: 1 Cairnsmore from Carsphairn

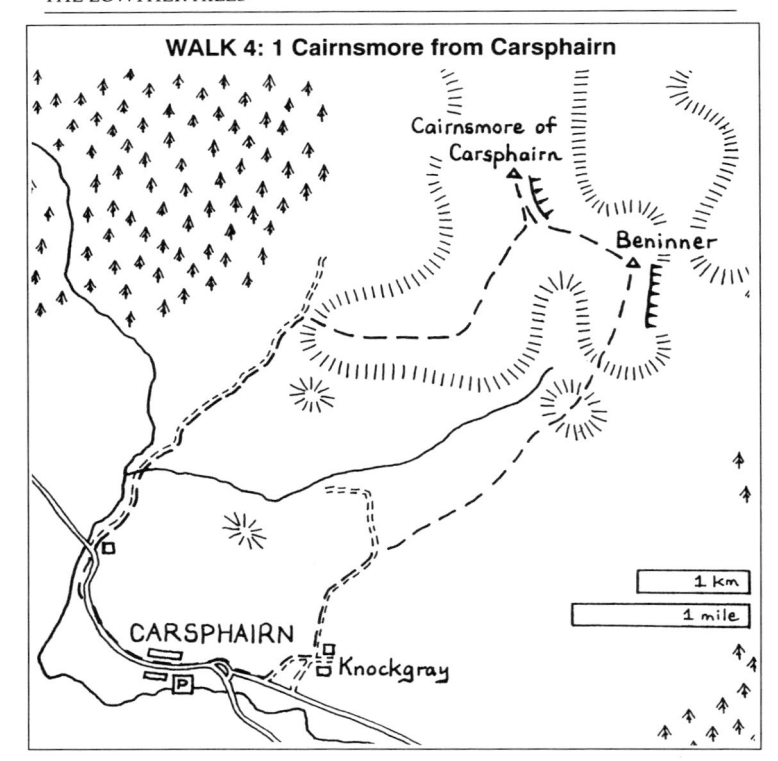

accompanying wall turns temporarily to fence to get through the wet bit: walkers must make of it the best they can. Grassy slopes lead up onto Knockwhirn, after which there is a short but steep descent. Go straight on up more grass, which gets shorter and then becomes moss and gravel at the summit cairn of Beninner.

Now we have fine views of the windfarm on Windy Standard, but also of the steep side of Cairnsmore, and of its boulder-peppered dome. From here on the surroundings are mountain, and granite mountain at that. Cairnsmore is entitled to consider itself a small cousin of a Cairngorm, with its own acre of tundra vegetation and stone. Descend gently to the inappropriately named Nick of the

Lochans, and up between the boulders to the summit with its cairn and trig point. On a clear day the view will stretch from England to Arran, with the Galloway Highlands occupying the sunset direction and the queer bump of Ailsa Craig. Two more queer but very distant bumps could even be Jura.

The descent shoulder is not visible from the summit - if mist is thick, a more straightforward descent can be made beside the wall that runs down from the trig point. Otherwise, head south until the shoulder appears below, and as boulders give way to short grass, a pleasant descent it is. A small path leads along the wall onto Dunool, with its little cairn. Go straight off the end, southwest, to go down steep but grassy slopes to the track below.

This leads down beside the small gorge of the Water of Deugh to reach the road at Green Well of Scotland. Turn left, taking the overgrown old road initially, and then walking the verge into Carsphairn.

Walk 4:2
* WINDY STANDARD and CAIRNSMORE
$12^{1/2}$ miles 3800ft (20km 1150m)
Rough grassy sides, pathless tops: hard

*The eastern side of Cairnsmore is the best. Here is an enclosed hollow, overlooked by rocky scarps and dotted with granite boulders. Threatened to north and south by creeping Christmas trees, and overlooked by the tall turbines of Windy Standard, it remains a precious patch of wild country. This walk passes among the turbines, and gains its star * for quality on condition that the walker is prepared to enjoy these imposing intrusions on the wilderness. Those who don't, or who want a shorter but equally wild approach to Cairnsmore, will use the short-cut variant given at the end of the walk.*

MAP: Landranger 77 (Dalmellington)

WINTER: In hard snow, the route can be taken in reverse and started with a direct ascent of Beninner Gairy. Alternatively, the shorter route can offer a direct ascent of Cairnsmore Gairy. Each of these, taken in crampons, could almost be considered as Winter Mountaineering Grade I.

The single-track road winds up beside the Water of Ken: a drive rendered gloomy by massed needle-trees.

START/FINISH: track end of the Craigengillan farm (GR 637948). Verge parking: do not obstruct entrance.

* * *

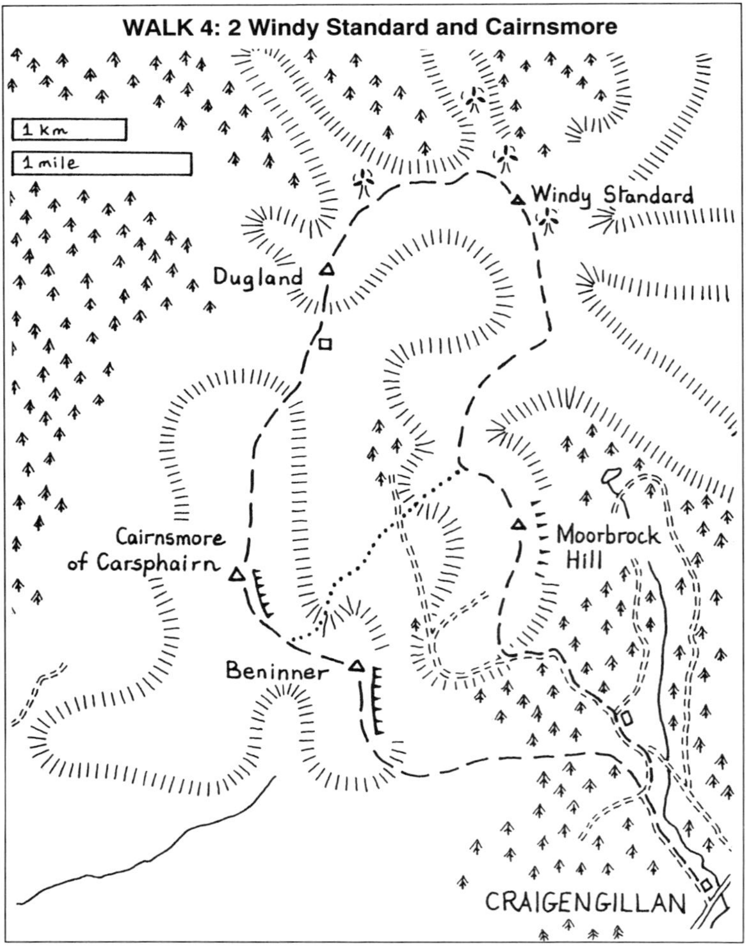
WALK 4: 2 Windy Standard and Cairnsmore
1 Km
1 mile
Windy Standard
Dugland
Cairnsmore
of Carsphairn
Moorbrock
Hill
Beninner
CRAIGENGILLAN

CARSPHAIRN HILLS

The track leads northwards, past the two small houses at Craigengillan. After a mile (1½ km) the main track turns left into the forest, and here turn right across a small stone bridge. The rough track leads across to the access track of Moorbrock farm.

Pass above the farm, and after the ford, turn left onto the uphill track. Just below the top of the trees, this contours away left; here leave it, and go up beside the Poltie Burn to reach the final tree. Grassy slopes lead straight up onto Moorbrock's summit plateau. The steep edge of Moorbrock Gairy on the right guides you forward to the unmarked summit.

Continue northwest to the second summit which, though lower, is marked with a cairn. (Here the short variant turns off.) It's a fairly steep drop into the col beyond. Rough ground leads to the summit of Keoch Rig. This unexciting top is marked by a single fence-post sinking into the boggy ground. Tramp northeast to meet a fence in the col beyond (GR 618003). Ignore a branch-fence that leads down right, towards Keoch Lane.

A double fence, one part old and collapsing, the other part even older and more collapsing, leads up out of the col. On the shoulder of Windy Standard is a further fence junction with a wide double-gate. Here turn left to follow the fence onto Windy Standard. 200yds along, and a little way below the fence, is the Deil's Putting Stane. Actually put by glacier rather than by satanic athlete, it's a frost-shattered boulder the size of a dinner-table.

Once on the plateau, you are confronted by the first of the 45 wind turbines. The chilly whirring noise adds to the bleakness of the spot, while the flashing blades, descending towards you at 100mph, add an element of scariness otherwise largely absent from these gentle hills. However, the gravel access road is no gain at all. This track runs to left of the summit trig point, so leave it and walk the sparse vegetation on its right. In late spring this is speckled with the white flowers of cloudberry, and in autumn with the cloudberry's red clustered berries.

The scruffy structure just south of the summit is a derelict weather station. Beyond it, views are to the rocky sides of Moorbrock, Beninner and Cairnsmore.

Descend westwards, crossing one windfarm track to join another in the col before Trostan Hill. The track passes two masts at the top

THE LOWTHER HILLS

of Polwhat Rig. As it turns away northwest, a gate leads out onto the summit of Dugland and the final windfarm outlier, a pole with an anemometer and photocell for counting sunlight.

For peak-baggers, Dugland is something of a curiosity: at 607m, it's the lowest 2000ft hill in the world! 607m is 1992ft, and Dugland is not expected to survive into the next edition of Donald's Tables. From the small cairn, go down steeply south to the small shelter at Clennoch. Somewhere on this descent is a memorial to a crashed pilot, but I've never managed to find it. The bothy at Clennoch is wonderfully situated but very small and has no stove or fireplace. From here you can, if necessary, escape up the Bow Burn to join the forest track that runs through the Moorbrock/Beninner gap back to Moorbrock farm.

Cross the Bow Burn to get started on the long north ridge that's the finest approach to Cairnsmore. The lower part has boulders and small outcrops of granite. At 650m the character changes as the ridge becomes a gently sloping plateau. Here are granite stones and gravel, and the closest to tundra vegetation that we get in southern Scotland - it could be a speck of Cairngorm plateau, transported 200 miles south. A cairn, the top end of a stone wall and a trig point mark Cairnsmore's summit, together with a sudden view down the long lochs of the Ken Valley and across to the Galloway Hills.

Descend south, then southeast, weaving between granite boulders with the sharp drop of Cairnsmore Gairy on the left. From the col go straight up to the cairn of Beninner.

Go down gently south on gravel that becomes short grass, and as the ground steepens, bend left (southeast). Too far left will involve you in the steep slopes of Beninner Gairy. Keep to right of these down to the 400m contour, where you reach the flat boggy ground below. Cross this eastwards, to join the Poldores Burn as it enters the forest. Across the burn a red metal gate leads through a wall, and then a grey metal gate through a fence. Go down the left bank of the burn on unplanted but fairly rough ground. The outward route is rejoined at the small bridge beside the first track junction.

* SHORTENED ROUTE: MOORBROCK to CAIRNSMORE
9 miles 2800ft (14km 850m): hard
This avoids the windfarm while still getting an ascent of the wild side of Cairnsmore.

From the second, lower, cairned, summit of Moorbrock, go down west into the broad col that is the Beninner/Moorbrock gap. Keep well above the trees at the head of the Bow Burn, and cross the forest track at the foot of the slope. Work round to right of the steep broken ground of Beninner Gairy, and ascend the bouldery slope between Beninner and Cairnsmore to the col.

At the col, turn right, up the rock-dotted slope to Cairnsmore summit.

Walk 4:3
EWE HILL
8 miles 2000ft (12½km 600m)
Steep rocky hillside, grassy ridges, path and track: hard

The flavour of this walk lies at the beginning. When you sucked an old-fashioned aniseed ball, the taste was actually all in the outer coating, and the later part of the sweet was a simple ball of hard sugar. In the same way, the streamside ascent of Ewe Hill is sharp enough that the taste of it will stay with you along the fairly ordinary grass ridges afterwards. The route twists around the central pivot of the Carsphairn Hills, the place where "Scaur and Euchan and Afton and Ken All meet up in ane hill end".

MAP: Landranger 77 (Dalmellington)

VARIANT: for those approaching from the west, a short return off Meikledodd is given so that the walk can be done from Lorg. This shortens the walk by 2 miles (3km). Those approaching from the east have the best of it: Scaur is a notably pretty little valley, which the upper Ken isn't.

SCRAMBLE VARIANT: "Ewes Hollow" is a more demanding line up the face of Ewes Hill. This earthy scramble is described after the main route.

COVENANTING SITES: The route could be extended south of the valley to take in two Covenanting sites. At Allan's Cairn is a monument to two people shot for attending an illegal conventicle. On the southwest flank of Altry Hill on the 440m contour is one of the places where

THE LOWTHER HILLS

conventicles were held. The Whig's Hole (GR 671000) is a grassy hollow in the hillside, unsuspected from below. The initial climb to Allan's Cairn is on forest road and the SU Way: the long ascent under the trees is rather depressing.

START/FINISH: The Scaur valley tarmac finally peters out at Polskeoch, and after 200yds of unsurfaced track is a locked gate with a small parking and turning area in front (GR 684022).

✽ ✽ ✽

There's a stile beside the locked gate. The track beyond crosses a stream to a junction with SU Way waymark pointing left. After 200yds, the track bends left. Here is a wooden SU Way signpost, with a third arm pointing into the forest and saying "Lorg". Follow this arm to find the start of a path at the back of the small quarry and hard standing area.

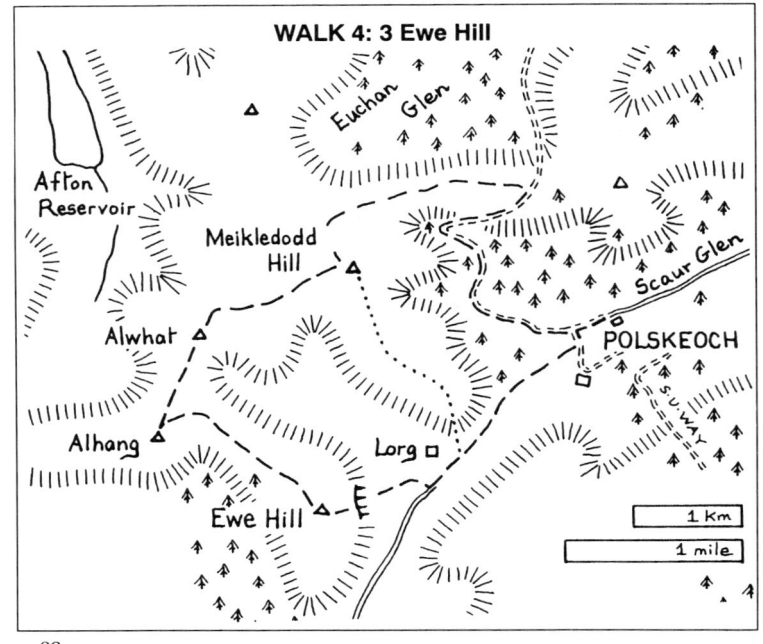

CARSPHAIRN HILLS

The path runs southwest along a narrow ride. The branches are starting to close in, and if one person in a hundred were to carry secateurs, they would earn the gratitude of the other ninety-nine. The path is just clear enough to be followable. If it's invisible due to snow, note that the correct ride either contours or gently descends, and side-rides slanting right, uphill, are wrong ones.

The path emerges onto open hillside at a wooden gate. Staying above the stream, it passes through the deep V-gap connecting Scaur with Ken. When the small house of Lorg comes into sight, cross a stile to left of stone walls onto the riverbank. Another stile lets you out onto the tarred road at its bridge over the Lorg Burn.

The east face of Ewe Hill is grass, bracken and rock, and is cut by two watercourses. The right-hand one is a deep stony hole that I've called "Ewes Hollow". The left-hand one, "Ewes Rill", is a series of small waterfalls. The ascent beside it is very steep, but rewarding.

Go up the left-hand (west) bank of the Lorg Burn to the second of two circular sheep fanks. Here a gate lets you through the fence on the left. Double back slightly to reach the foot of Ewes Rill (GR 666007).

Go up the grassy bank immediately to left of the stream, passing the first four or five waterfalls. Where a stony gully comes down from the left, cross the bottom of it by working across to the stream side.

At the top of the next waterfall is a clump of low-growing juniper. Pass to left of this midget forest and traverse to right, above it, to cross the stream at the foot of the final waterfall. Go up the slope of mixed earth and rock to right of the fall. The stream now runs up much less steeply, inside a grassy hollow between low rock walls, and this makes a charming finish to the interesting bit. The stream runs up into grassy slopes directly below the summit of Ewe Hill. The small summit cairn has been lovingly wrapped in coils of rusting fence wire.

Follow the fence northwest, over the second summit of Ewe Hill. It is ordinary grass ridge, but the westward view manages to arrange the five least-gentle slopes of the Carsphairns one behind the other. Backlit by an afternoon sun, and given the correct amount of heat-haze, the effect is mildly mountainous. At the far side of the damp col the fence divides. The right fork (northwards) is a short-

THE LOWTHER HILLS

cut to Alwhat. The main route follows the left-hand fence, up into the col marked as "source of the Afton" and then left along a ridgeline fence. The summit of Alhang is a three-stone cairn on the Glenkens side of the fence. On the other side of it is a view down to the Afton Reservoir.

Return along the fence into the col and up onto grassy Alwhat. The fence still guides along the short drop and climb onto Meikledodd; there are quad bike wheelmarks nearby on the left. At the fence junction high on Meikledodd, turn right. The summit, which is unmarked, is to left of this new fence. Here you look northwards into the Euchan valley and try to decide which hill end is the exact one where the four valleys meet. (Those making their return to Lorg continue along this fence.)

Return northwards along the fence for 500yds to where four fences meet - and three counties, for this is the common point of Ayrshire, Dumfriesshire and the Stewartry of Kirkcudbright. Bear right, northeast, along a fence that's no longer stockproof. It leads along the top of Ryegrain Rig to meet the forest road at the point where it crosses from Euchan to Scaur. This is the "Heads of the Valleys Road", which makes a long and very hilly bike ride connecting four valleys.

Our walk meets this road at its highest point, and turns right for the bendy descent to Polskeoch.

VARIANT: EWES HOLLOW

A harsh scramble, grade 1, though actual difficulties are steep earth and grass. A striking situation, it would make a short but sporting ascent if it were ever to get good snow in it.

Ewes Hollow is the northern one of two streams running down the east face of Ewe Hill (GR 666009). Go up the stream into the deep stony chasm. The stream bed gives a couple of short pitches, which are preferable to the steep grass alongside. The walls of the chasm now rise above. Ignore the first dry gully forking left. The stream cascades down the vertical wall on the right, and here a second dry gully forks left. This is the one to take, either on the steep loose scree of its floor or steep grass just to the left.

CARSPHAIRN HILLS

VARIANT FINISH: for those starting from Lorg
Start from an area of hardened verge just before the bridge over the Lorg Burn (GR 668006).

Follow the main walk up Ewe Hill and as far as Meikledodd's summit. Continue along the fence, southeast, over Lorg Hill. At the 650m contour the fence bends left, east. Here leave it and descend southeast, then south. The ground steepens, to give a view down onto the roof of Lorg House.

Go down the steep spur. Pass left of the walled enclosures to a small stile leading onto the riverbank. A second stile lets you onto the road at the start-point.

Walk 4:4
** BLACKCRAIG and BLACKLORG from AFTON
8 miles 2400ft (13km 700m)
Grassy, pathless: moderate

Robert Burns' "Sweet Afton" refers to the wooded lower glen. The upper part is a rocky hollow among grassy hills. This walk makes the most of the rocky bits. Tiny episodes of rock-scrambling are available at William's Castle, and also on the Variant Route at the Giant's Cave. Man's hand assists Nature in the large and pleasing reservoir, the large and almost equally pleasing earth-works of its dam wall. While some are pleased, some displeased, by the forty tall wind turbines that overlook the walk from the western side of the valley.

MAP: Landranger 77 (Dalmellington)

VARIANT: the exploration of the Giant's Cave is a very short scramble, followed by a demanding ascent of steep ground.

START/FINISH: on hard verge of the valley road at any point after the track end of Blackcraig farm (GR 632081)

❉ ❉ ❉

The Blackcraig farm track crosses the wooded valley bottom. Pass to left of all buildings at Blackcraig farm, and head uphill with a narrow plantation on the right. At the plantation top will be found the beginning of the old green track.

This goes up to left of the main stream, which has waterfalls.

THE LOWTHER HILLS

```
WALK 4: 4 Blackcraig, Blacklorg from Afton
```

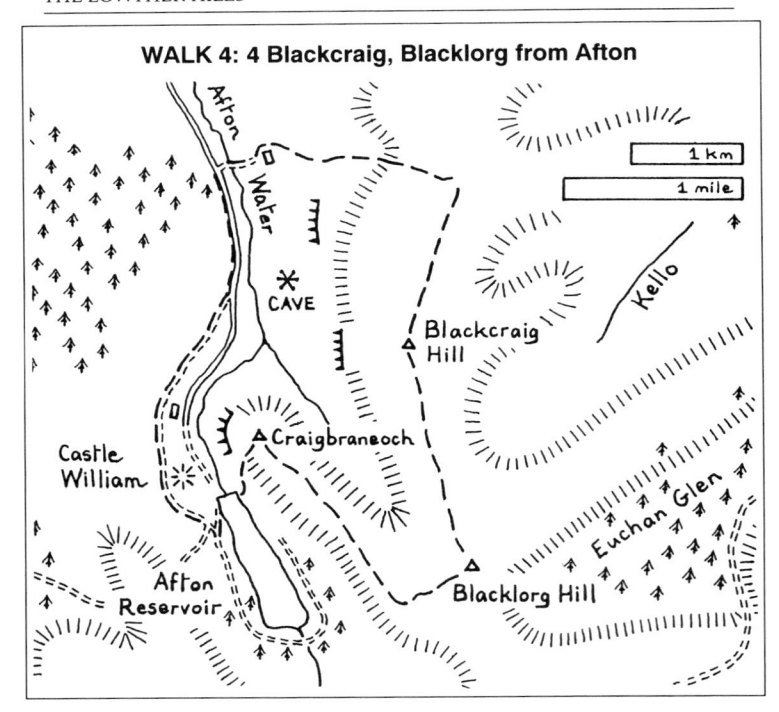

There are fine views both up and down the valley of the Sweet Afton: the picnic spot of Robert Burns and his friends was passed on the road in. (Burns' picnics were largely alcoholic ones.) The enjoyable wide path becomes boggy for 100yds - its ancient drainage having broken down - then reaches more level ground at a cairn. After another 100yds it reaches the gate and fence at the pass leading over towards the Kello Water.

(The path continuing ahead does make a pleasant descent into the Kello valley, but beware! Alongside this path, at Dunside, is a quarry where explosions take place. Metals of different melting points, such as mild steel and stainless steel, are welded together by means of dynamite.)

Our current route turns off right, before the gate, and follows the fence up onto Blackcraig Hill. Blackcraig's summit plateau is a bouldery place, wilder than any of the surrounding grass. Its rock-hummocks make it confusing in mist. Follow the fence up onto the rocky place, crossing a side-fence leading down right, and then seeking the trig point about 50yds to right of the fence.

Leave the trig point northeast, passing the summit cairn, and rejoining the fence. The fence leads down the broad slope to the col, which is a damp one with some peat hags. These can be avoided on the right.

Continue, with only occasional remains of a fence largely removed, up the slope to Blacklorg Hill. Three fences meet at this summit. The one to the right is accompanied by the remains of a stone dyke, and this is the one to follow over Cannock Hill.

In the col beyond Cannock Hill, the fence turns away left, to the reservoir - there's a gate at the corner if you've ended on the wrong side of it. Continue ahead (northwest) to the rocky summit of Craigbraneoch Hill (575m). This, though unworthy of a name on the Landranger map, is the finest of the Afton peaks and a place to linger, with views down the vale of Sweet Afton to the Ayrshire plain. Or you can sit and look across the reservoir to where the wind turbines in their long row go round and round and round...

Descend southwest, keeping to left of craggy ground. Enter the small plantation at its left-hand end, and pass through it to the shore of the reservoir. Cross the dam.

At the dam's western end, a pine-needle track leads left through trees. After 50yds, a higher track doubles back right, to escape from the forest and join another. Walking down-valley on this combined track, you see the rock-lump of William's Castle just below. If the giant of the variant route was satisfied with a very small cave, William is happy with a very small castle. Its western wall has a short scramble to the summit picnic spot. Just to the south is the small but pointed William's Pinnacle. Careful camera-angles make this into somewhere in the Swiss Alps. Because of the overhang, the pinnacle is easier to climb up than to climb back down.

On the way back to the track, a small gorge is crossed or avoided. The track runs down the valley, passing above Craigdarroch farm and joining the tarred road ¾ mile (1km) short of the start-point.

THE LOWTHER HILLS

VARIANT: GIANT'S CAVE
This variant takes the steep face of Blackcraig direct, to visit the cave refuge of a very small giant.

Drive past the Blackcraig farm road, to park ½ mile (¾km) further on, where the verge on the left is wide and hard. A stream, marked on Landranger, runs down the face of Blackcraig. It drips through the cave, which can be seen from the roadside and is at GR 638070.

Just before a narrow plantation below the road, a gate leads down into pasture. The Afton Water can be paddled through near the field's right-hand corner. Go up immediately to right of the stream. A few feet of scrambling up the stream bed lead into the cave. Refuge? It's the very small giant's shower cubicle.

Reverse the short scramble, and go up to right of the stream. A fence runs uphill on the left. Where the fence reaches the summit plateau, turn right, along the crossing fence, to find the trig point and cairn at Blackcraig's summit.

Walk 4:5
EUCHAN TOP with BLACKLORG HILL
10 miles 1800ft (16km 550m)
Pathless rough grass: hard

This walk is over pathless, and rather damp, tussocks. It has a certain grim remoteness that is not unattractive.

MAP: Landranger 77 (Dalmellington)

EXTENSION: Can be combined with Walk 4:6 for 20 miles (32km) of rough tramping.

The Euchan road is single-track, with widely-spaced passing places, and a high and steep drop alongside. It is not for nervous reversers. Park before the final cattle grid and the bridge to Glenglass, at the foot of the gated forest road.

START/FINISH: Euchan road top (GR 709065)

※　※　※

A forest road starts at a locked gate, with stile alongside. It passes above Euchanbank, and after 1¼ miles (2km) the waters of the

CARSPHAIRN HILLS

WALK 4: 5 Euchan Top with Blacklorg Hill

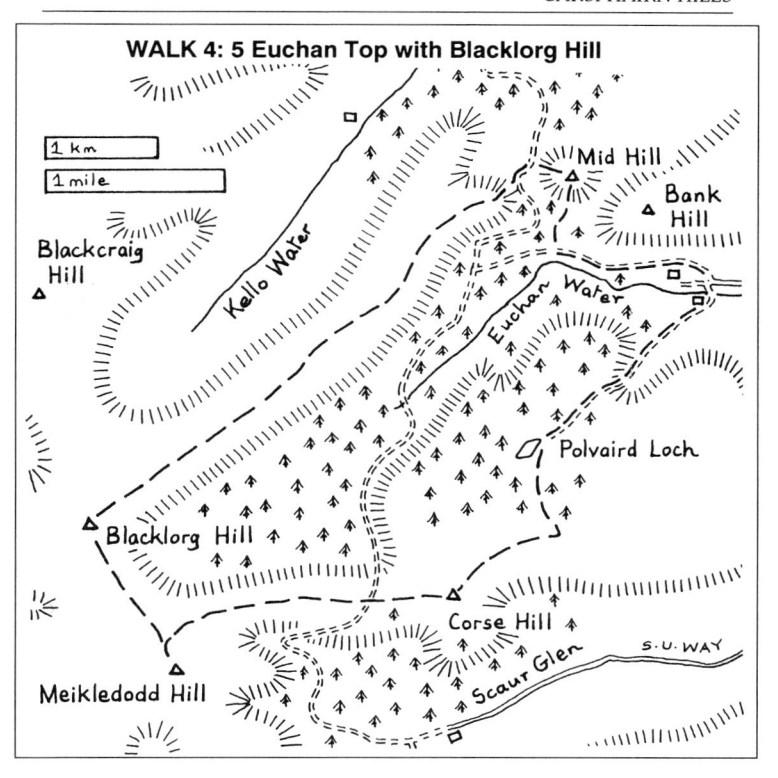

Poltallan Burn flow across it. Turn right, and go up the stream, with a stone wall alongside. After passing a few small waterfalls, the wall turns off right: a small gorge, with rowan trees, is just above. Turn off along the wall, to emerge onto open grass at the foot of Mid Hill. Go up this, very steeply.

At the top of Mid Hill turn left over flat ground to another forest road, and turn left along this to recross the Poltallan Burn. Before the gate where the road re-enters trees, head up right, to reach Well Hill. After a sharp dip, the wide grass ridge continues to the 568m spotheight. Here a fence arrives from the right, and is followed along the ridge. The going gradually becomes easier as height is gained,

THE LOWTHER HILLS

becoming quite pleasant on the final pull to Blacklorg Hill.

Turn sharp left, and follow another fence down into the grassy col. Avid peak-baggers can continue up the fence to Meikledodd, before returning for 400yds to the fence junction that is the common boundary point of Ayrshire, Kirkcudbright and Dumfries.

Turn sharp left, along a fence now lacking wire, descending gently and then climbing gently to the 600m top of Ryegrain Rig. The fence continues, to reach the forest road that climbs from the right out of the Scaur Valley.

Turn left down this track. It could be used as a quick finish to the walk. (After its first descent it crosses the burn. After another mile (1^1/$_2$km), it forks: the lower, right-hand, branch rejoins the outward route at the Poltallan Burn.)

But if you have an appetite for more of the rough stuff, follow the track towards Euchan for just 100yds, before striking off to a gate on the right. A fence leads up the grassy slope to the crumbling trig point of Corse Hill. Stay with the main ridgeline, and the fence, for ^{3}/$_4$ mile (1km), as far as the anemometer mast on Rough Shoulder.

Here forest runs up to the ridgeline fence. At the mast, a ride runs into the trees, sharply back left. It has faint wheelmarks to aid passage, and runs northwest, then bends right to run north. At a ride junction fork slightly left, to keep on the north bearing, and reach Polvaird Loch.

Follow the edge of the trees to the right for 200yds, to the top of a rough track. This has a fine outlook; watch out for roe deer among the trees. The track slants down the steep flank of Cruffel to the start-point of the walk.

Walk 4:6
EUCHAN BOTTOM: CLOUD HILL and EUCHAN WATER
14 miles 1500ft (22km 450m)
Path, track, road and grassy ridge: easy/moderate

At one point this walk has been damaged by the hand of man: the high lochan of Polvaird, planted all around with dismal spruce. Elsewhere, however, the rough ridge-top has been tamed and made pleasant by the

---

Walkers above the Needle's Eye (Walk 5:7)

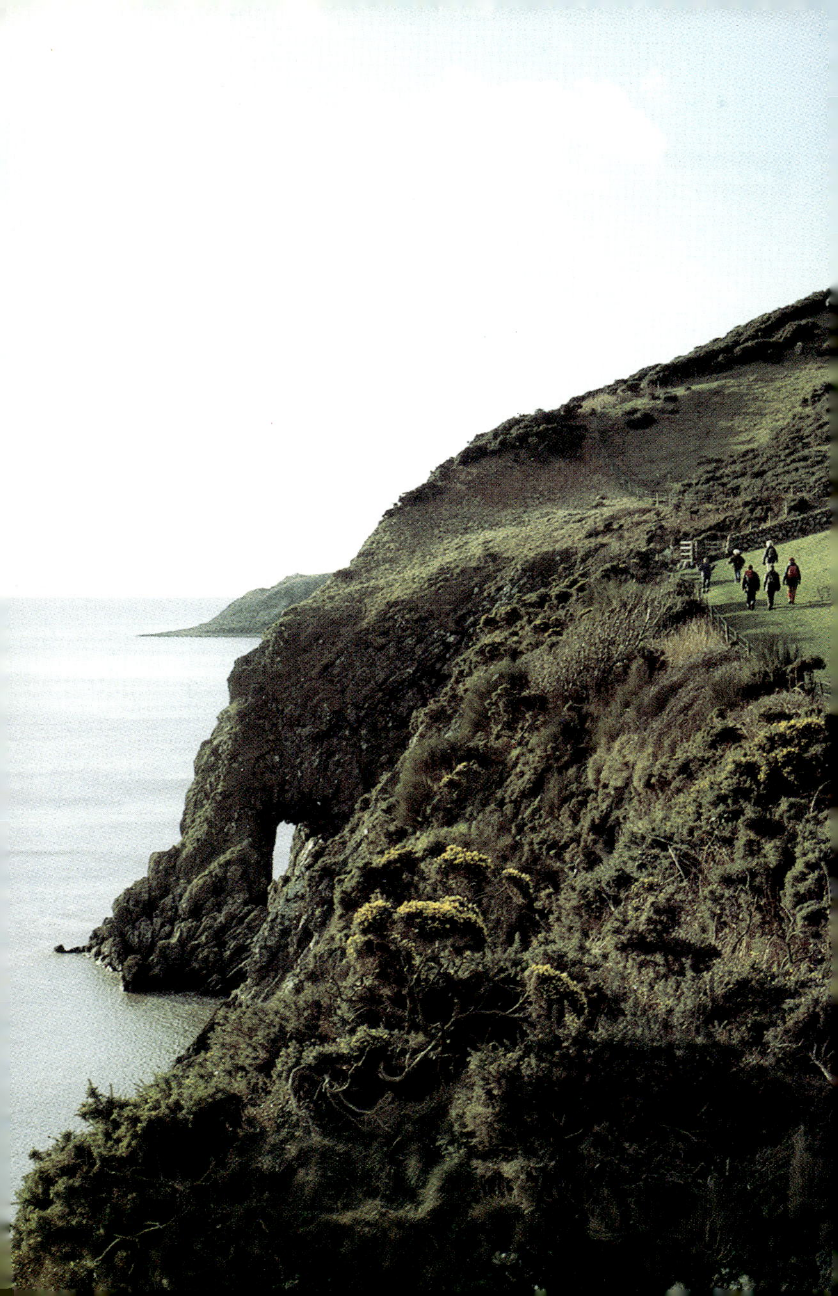

Looking down Sweet Afton from Craigbraneoch Hill (Walk 4:4)
Criffel from Loch Kindar (Walks 5:1, 5:2, 5:3)

CARSPHAIRN HILLS

shepherd's quad bike, and the riverside path has been created out of nettlebed by the job creation team. The walk includes 2 miles (3½km) of road - but it is pleasant, even stimulating, road. It would, though, be a mistake to stay on road all the way down the Euchan: the woods and riverside at the end are the remedy of what might otherwise be an austere outing.

MAPS: Both Landranger 77 (Dalmellington) and Landranger 78 (Nithsdale)

EXTENSION: combine this with Walk 4:5 for 20 miles (32km) of rough tramping. The combined route follows this walk to Rough Shoulder and then reverses Walk 4:5. After the steep descent of Mid Hill, a diversion can be made over Bank Hill and Black Hill, following ridgeline fences to descend forest edge to the Water Works. Thus a steep-sided, pool-topped bonus hill replaces a mile of road.

START/FINISH: Sanquhar. In dry weather, there is verge parking near Ulzieside (do not obstruct farm entrances): otherwise, a convenient car park is at the Nith Bridge (GR 776096).

※ ※ ※

Cross the Nith Bridge, and turn left for ¾ mile (1km) to Ulzieside farm. The track to right of the farm buildings is part of the Southern Upland Way. It runs uphill to a gate, and then bends to the right. Here we and the SU Way continue ahead, uphill with a wall on the left, to a stile. Go round a walled sheep-pen to a hidden ladderstile on the left.

Contour across rough boggy ground. There are occasional waymarks, but the path is small and indistinct, showing how little used is Scotland's longest Long Distance Path. Pass above a railed enclosure to the footbridge over the Whing Burn, then head up the broad grassy ridge alongside this stream. There are widely-spaced waymarks, but the sheep rub against them and knock them over.

The grassy knoll at Whing Head has a small marker-stone. Here the path turns right to a stile, then slants down into the pass over the main ridge. Do not cross the ladderstile, but turn right, alongside the wall, and pass over several rocky knolls - the last and highest of them is Cloud Hill.

Now the wall alongside becomes a low fence. Step over it, and continue alongside it on the wheelmarks of a quad bike. The way

THE LOWTHER HILLS

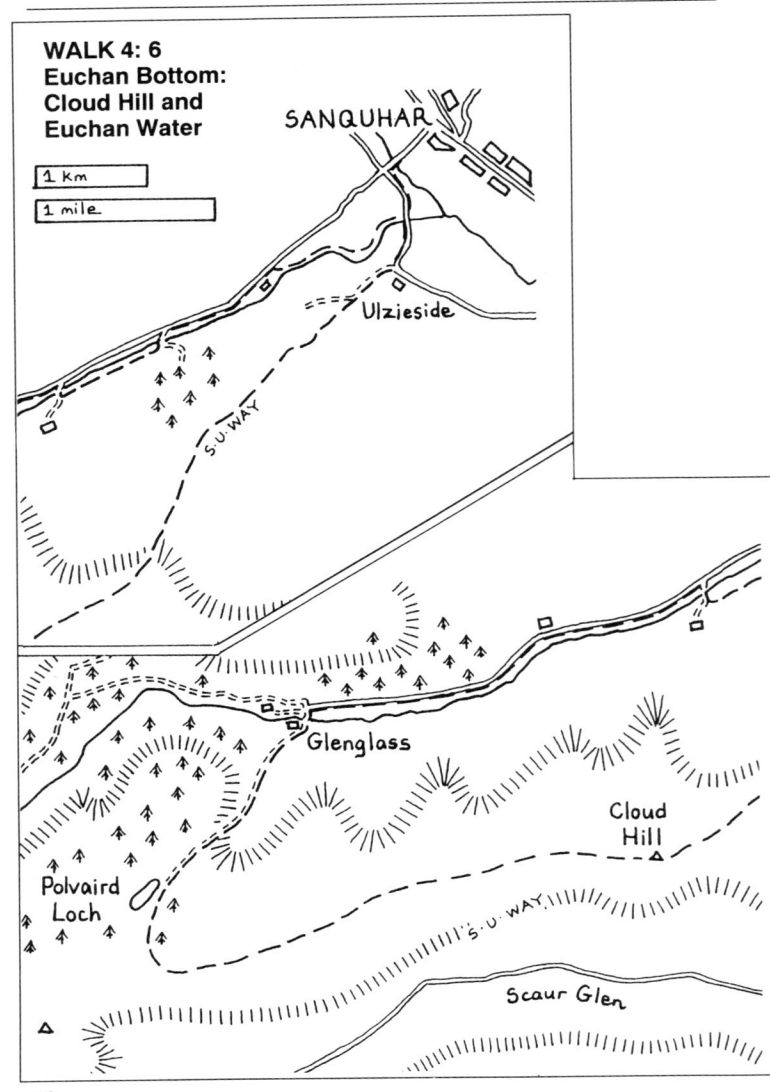

CARSPHAIRN HILLS

here overlooks the deep, lonely valley of the Scaur Water. Views back are to Glenwhargen Craig and Cairnkinna (Walk 4:7). The fence changes to a wall again, and then, at spot-height 503m, bends away to north, but a fence continues, guiding along the ridge line.

After another 2 miles (3km), trees arrive at the right-hand side of the fence. Go up alongside them onto Rough Shoulder. Here is an anemometer mast, assessing the site for a possible wind-farm. The mast is exactly at the 558m spot-height.

Turn right along the forest top for 200yds, passing the mast, to a ride into the forest. (The beginning of the ride is exactly north of the mast.) The ride runs northwest, then north: it neither gains nor loses height, and has wheelmarks. After passing through a ruined gateway, take the left-hand ride, to the head of Polvaird Loch.

This is, in fact, an unusually large peat-pool, having neither feeder stream nor outflow. The usual legends apply: it is said to be bottomless (the depth is about 3m/10ft) and never to freeze over (I have skied across it).

Follow the tree-edge on the right to find the top of the track that descends quite steeply to Glenglass cottage.

Turn right along the valley road, and follow it, or the grass alongside, for 2 miles (3½km). A particularly bumpy section was laid, according to a valley resident, on top of packed snow. After the waterworks the road becomes high and exposed, above a steep-sided wooded valley. When the track to Glenmaddie is seen below, descend through the bracken and cross its bridge.

Turn left after the sheep pens, onto a well-graded track. This is the former valley road, dating back to when thirty-seven households inhabited the Euchan. It descends into the riverside wood, then bends left to cross the river and rejoin the tarred road.

Continue down the road for a sharp descent, and after Old Barr turn right, through a narrow gate. The path crosses a field to the Euchan. It runs downstream through woods, and poises itself above the river. Two waterfalls below the path are a good viewpoint for leaping salmon at the appropriate season. The observant, and even the unobservant, may spot the change in the rocks, and in the character of the stream. Instead of lumpy grey shale, we now have flat slabs of pink sandstone.

The path passes a healing spring of rusty water, to reach the road. Turn left, back to the Nith Bridge.

Glenwhargen Craig and Cairnkinna from Cloud Hill

Walk 4:7
* GLENWHARGEN CRAIG and CAIRNKINNA
8 miles 1800ft (13km 700m)
Scramble Grade 2, rough grassy hilltops: moderate/hard

Apart from some granite in Galloway, Glenwhargen is the closest the Southern Uplands gets to a climbing crag. The scramble is not technically difficult, but it is serious and exposed, on rock with some vegetable cover that may be loose in places. There are few if any belays, and a rope will not be particularly useful (except where one member of the party is strong and confident and the other isn't). The route should be avoided during the nesting season for birds of prey.

A rough grassy ridge gives fine views down into Scaur, and leads to a fine final summit. Cairnkinna has a high, impressively-built cairn and a view of all Nithsdale.

MAP: Landranger 78 (Nithsdale)

START/FINISH: a quarry lay-by to right of the Scaur Valley road 400yds past Chanlockfoot (GR 787004)

❊ ❊ ❊

CARSPHAIRN HILLS

Walk up the road for 150yds. A kissing-gate on the left leads to the riverside at pools, waterfalls and a small jutting crag: a good place to leave the non-hillwalking family members. Follow the riverbank to a second gate back onto the road.

Go up the road for 2 miles (3km), passing below the small Hallscaur Craig to the larger and impressive Glenwhargen one. This is divided by a narrow, shallow gully that bends left, then back right above. Make a way up screes to the bottom of this gully.

Scramble up the gully bed, or fairly clean rocks immediately to its right, to where it bends left. Now strike up right, on rock and grass, to the crest of the spur. This goes up, mostly on rock rather than plant life, at a moderate angle to a steep final tower.

The tower is easier than it looks. A ledge traverses left

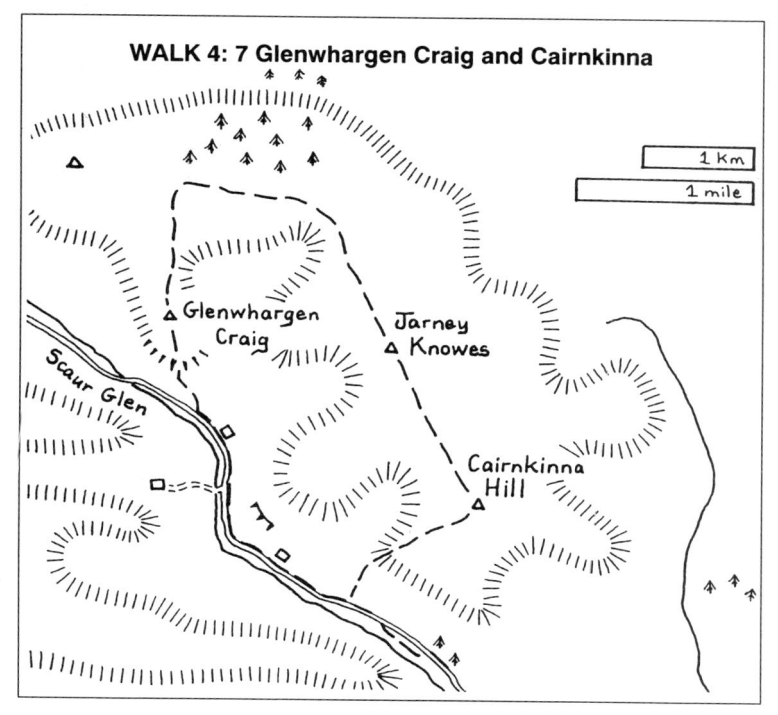

THE LOWTHER HILLS

immediately below the steep wall, and then a slanting gangway leads back up to right. Easier ground leads to the crag's summit lump, overlooking Scaur Valley.

Head north, over the rough-tussocked hill, towards the main ridge a mile away. The 482m summit is impossible to pin down, and easier going is offered by wheelmarks around the right-hand rim of the hill. These wheelmarks lead down slightly right to a gate at the stream crossing before Shiel Hill (GR 766043). Leave the wheelmarks to reach the fence at forest edge ahead.

Turn right along the fence, crossing the undistinguished summit of Shiel Hill without noticing it and dropping into a col: the metal gate here is the line of an ancient way between Scaur and Nith that's no longer traceable on the ground. Turn right at a fence junction to reach Jarney Knowes - with increasing height, the grass underfoot is becoming less rough.

At a second fence junction on Black Rig (509m), head out away from the fences into the wide col before Cairnkinna. Keep to the right-hand side of the col for drier ground. Paths and wheelmarks lead up to the summit. A five-strand electric fence protects the trig point and the cairn - it will be necessary to use one of the fence-techniques described in the Introduction (or follow the fence to the right, eventually to find a gate).

The cairn itself is a beehive structure some 10ft (3m) high. It is not scheduled as an ancient monument, and is presumably Victorian. Sadly, people attempting to climb it have broken the stonework and it is beginning to collapse.

Turn southwest, alongside the fence, on wheelmarks. A gate in this fence opens onto the top of the steep spur that leads down to the foot of the Carlinstane Burn. The spur, though steep, is rocks and grass, with intimate valley views and a comfortable descent - be careful not to end up on steep stones to left, above the valley road.

At the foot of the hill turn left, above a stone wall, to rejoin the road ¹/₂ mile (1km) from the start-point.

Galloway Hills from the Glenkens

Walkers based in the Glenkens will not want to restrict themselves to Cairnsmore, when the Galloway Hills are just across the valley. *Walking the Galloway Hills* (Paddy Dillon) approaches these hills

CARSPHAIRN HILLS

from the exciting granite country beyond. So it is worth mentioning here that the long and very enjoyable ridge walk of the Rhinns of Kells can also be approached from the east.

The starting point is the small car park at Forrest Lodge (GR 552862). From here, marked trails lead out to the top edge of the plantations at various convenient points: below Meikle Lump (GR 539838), above Loch Dungeon (GR 515852) and at the Folk Burn below Corserine (GR 517873). You can also make a way onto Cairnsgarroch from the forest road corner at GR 521890.

There is some scrambling on the rocky eastern slope of Milldown, above Loch Dungeon.

Climbing William's Pinnacle
(Walk 4:4)

5: Solway Coast

The Solway Coast is like Cornwall, only less crowded and colder. Here are golden beaches, and rugged clifftops, and views to the Lake District on the other side. Here are seaside villages of white-painted stone. Here also are wide mudflats that glisten under a winter sun like stranded jellyfish. It's a shoreline with a history of smuggling, and a present-day sport of flounder tramping (which is attempting to catch flatfish in mud with your toes).

Here also are three granite hills. They are small, but savage, covered in grey speckled boulders, black peat and heather. Criffel and Screel are the high points of the present section: the following one will be devoted to Cairnsmore of Fleet.

Walk 5:1
** CRIFFEL from NEW ABBEY
7 miles 2000ft (11km 600m)
Paths, easy/moderate

The granite lump of Criffel stands 1872ft (570m) above the Nith estuary. It often enjoys better weather than inland hills (but sometimes worse, of course). On a clear day its views include countryside, seaside, and the mountains of England across gleaming Solway mud. The striking village of New Abbey, followed by pleasantly gentle slopes, make this my favourite ascent of Criffel, even though you have to come back the same way.

The path is damp, and can be muddy after rain or after the annual Criffel Hill Race in mid-March. The winner of that race completes this route in under 50 minutes!

MAP: Landranger 84 (Dumfries)

ALTERNATIVE: The walk starts and ends with ½ mile (1km) of tarred lane. For a track and field alternative, use Walk 5:2 (Waterloo Monument) to and from Mid Glen.

START/FINISH: Criffel Inn, New Abbey (GR 963663). Or car park at the Abbey itself.

❉ ❉ ❉

SOLWAY COAST

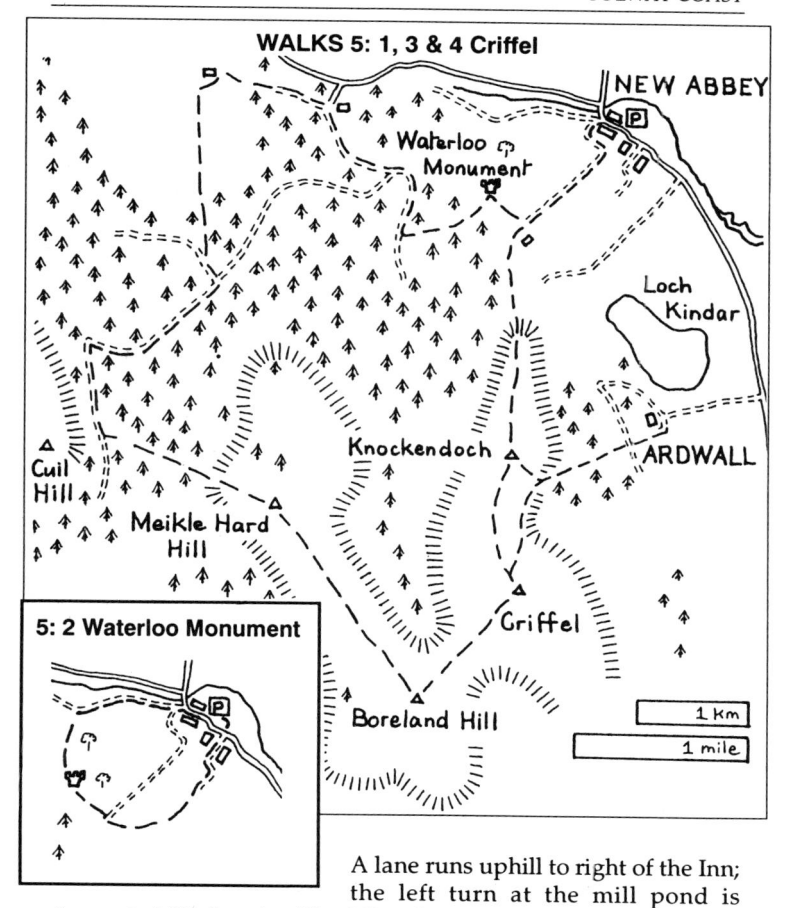

WALKS 5: 1, 3 & 4 Criffel

NEW ABBEY

Waterloo Monument

Loch Kindar

Cuil Hill

Meikle Hard Hill

Knockendoch

ARDWALL

Criffel

Boreland Hill

1 Km
1 mile

5: 2 Waterloo Monument

A lane runs uphill to right of the Inn; the left turn at the mill pond is signposted "Pedestrian Way Waterloo Monument". Stone steps in the embankment above the road lead to a kissing-gate. Go up the edge of a field to another kissing-gate. A gap in the stone wall lets you back onto the lane above its zigzag.

At Mid Glen the lane becomes track. It continues to the left, signposted "Criffel", across a stream and towards two newly-built

THE LOWTHER HILLS

Douglas' Cairn at Criffel Summit

houses. At the gate to the second house, take a path on the right. This winds between gorsy knolls for ¼ mile (400m) to join an unsurfaced road. Follow this uphill for 100yds. Short-cut across the track's sharp left bend, and where it turns back right continue ahead on a path. The path slants up through young trees to join a stone wall.

The path goes directly uphill alongside the wall. It crosses a stile onto open hill at the foot of the steep final slope. The path is plain, but can be muddy. On the final approach to Knockendoch, granite boulders start to appear, and so does a fine view across the Solway.

The path bends right past the cairn, descends briefly, and continues southwestward across the small col. It contours up the left-hand (east) side of Criffel's northern spur. The final slope is taken direct.

Criffel's summit has granite boulders, a trig point, a large cairn and wide views inland and out to sea. The nearest point of high ground is Queensberry, 23 miles (37km) away; the next nearest is Skiddaw, 26 miles (42km) away and in a different country across the sea. On a crisp winter's day, the Isle of Man and even the Irish hills will be visible.

SOLWAY COAST

The path down starts from the cairn, not the trig pillar, to cross the low remains of a stone wall. 50yds from the summit it appears to divide in two, but beware as the right half is actually a branch-path that bends away down the eastern slopes to Ardwall (Walk 5:4).

Follow the outward route back over Knockendoch to Mid Glen. Here you can divert onto Walk 5:2 to the Waterloo Monument: an enjoyable extension to the walk. Otherwise, return down the lane to New Abbey.

Walk 5:2
* WATERLOO MONUMENT
3 miles 500ft (5km 150m)
Paths and tracks but a steep ascent: moderate
See map for Walk 5:1 p105

A pleasant short walk leads to the ascent of a spectacular stone tower. The steep spiral stair and the unprotected summit of the Waterloo Monument are no place for the faint-hearted. The more irresponsible sort of ten-year-old will love it; I'd be inclined to treat the place as an exposed scramble, and rope them up.

MAP: Landranger 84 (Dumfries)

ALTERNATIVE: The walk can be made slightly shorter by replacing the first mile of track and field with the lane to Mid Glen. This is the start of Walk 5:1.

START/FINISH: The Abbey car park (GR 965662)

❄   ❄   ❄

The beautiful sandstone abbey was founded by Devorgilla, Lady Balliol, in 1273, and she is buried here along with the embalmed heart of her husband John de Balliol. Their son John Balliol was briefly king of Scotland, known as Toom Tabard (empty coat) as he was a mere puppet of the English king Edward I. She herself was more dynamic, founding Balliol College at Oxford and building the first bridge over the Nith at Dumfries as well as this fine abbey.

You don't have to pay to enter the abbey's graveyard. Go through this, to left of the abbey, to its back left corner, and take a

Sweetheart Abbey

path running to the left. Steps lead down to a field-edge path, and this is followed to the right through one field. Now turn right onto a smaller path past playing fields. This leads through a gap between houses onto the A710 road.

Follow the road to the left as far as the Abbey Filling Station, then turn right into a residential street opposite. Ignoring side streets on both sides, follow the street round a bend to the right, to the driveway of Barbeth House.

Enter the driveway through white gates, passing a sign "Barbeth, Private Road" (it is an asserted right-of-way for walkers). As the driveway turns right, continue ahead on a gate marked "No Vehicles Beyond this Point". The track leads through two more gates. These gates are heavy and badly hung, so that some strength is required to open them. At the same time, barbed wire is wound to prevent climbing over. Walkers for whom this may be a problem can take the lane of Walk 5:1 to reach Mid Glen.

The track passes along the edge of a small pine plantation (GR 963652). A fourth gate, a concrete bridge, and a fifth gate lead into an open field. The sixth gate enters the forestry plantation opposite.

SOLWAY COAST

A forest road leads forward, but ignore it and turn right, along the edge of the trees, on a path that heads for the skyline tower of the Waterloo Monument. After 300yds go through a seventh gate into open field. The path, a faint trod, crosses the field to a plain wooden gate. This opens onto the end of the lane at Mid Glen. Turn right to cross the small stream.

On the left is a sign "Waterloo Monument". After a derelict stile, a slightly raised path leads through woodland. It goes straight across a faint green track and then up a steep ascent with rough stone steps. The base of the monument is a fine place to linger and enjoy views back to the Abbey and southwards across Loch Kindar to the Solway and England.

A very narrow and steep spiral stair leads up inside the tower to its top, which has no parapet. Ascending and descending parties will have difficulty in passing each other. (The ascender should take the steeper inside of the stair.)

Behind the tower, a path slants down northwards through the plantation, while a third, waymarked path leads southwestwards into the trees. (That route returns to New Abbey by way of the Solway Fishery and is longer but less interesting.) Descend northwards on the pine-needle path. Where a green track crosses turn left for just 20yds, then back right onto the descending path; there are some waymarks here, although not particularly helpful ones. At the foot of the slope the path meets but does not cross a small stream (GR 951662), then bends right, north-east. It passes through pleasant woods to meet the Carsegowan farm track. A cautious noticeboard warns of ruts in the track.

Turn right, to reach New Abbey after $1/2$ mile ($3/4$km). The track passes among the scented stacks of Kingan's hardwood sawmill to arrive below the millpond.

THE LOWTHER HILLS

Walk 5:3
BORELAND HILL and CRIFFEL from NEW ABBEY
11 miles 2600ft (18km 800m)
Forest road and rough hillside: hard
See map with Walk 5:1 p105

The Forestry Commission has established a long-distance route from Caulkerbush to Mabie. Their route is almost entirely on forest road, so is not included here. However, part of it can be used to pass through the plantations to the grim and pathless outliers on the flank of Criffel.

Forgotten tracks around Kinharvie are pleasant, but the route also involves 2½ miles (4km) of that forest road. Contrariwise, the crossing from Boreland Hill to Criffel is very rough heather and grass. As well as being longer than the direct route, this one is, then, very varied. Its main advantage, though, is that the rough tracks, the overhanging trees and the rough heather make the final descent of the north ridge even more pleasant by contrast.

MAP: Landranger 84 (Dumfries)

START/FINISH: Mid Glen (GR 957654): small parking area. Or use Walk 5:2 (backwards) to start from New Abbey.

❊   ❊   ❊

A signpost indicates the path through the wood to the steep boulder steps and the Waterloo Monument. Of the paths into the plantation from the Monument, take the southward one "New Abbey by Solway Fishery".

The path is intermittently waymarked. It follows a ride slightly west of south, then turns right onto a southwestward one that contours and descends gently to meet a forest road (GR 945653). Turn right, downhill, continuing right and downhill at a junction (or branching left to by-pass Kinharvie). The right-hand track leads down to the bridge at the entrance to the Solway Fishery.

At this crossroads turn left. Follow the forest road through Kinharvie plantation to its end. An unused track continues ahead to leave the plantation by a handsome joiner-made gate. (Heave this piece of woodwork aside rather than risking damage by climbing over it.)

A faint track runs across a bridge to Kinharvie. Turn left through

SOLWAY COAST

the farmyard to a gate onto an uphill track. Follow this through a wood of beech and oak, with the Kinharvie Burn on the left. Soon you emerge onto newly-planted hill. Take a left fork towards a bridge. Do not, however, cross this bridge, but continue uphill with the stream still on your left.

Pass the ruined Hayfield House, and enter forest by a wooden gate. Planted larches on the right contrast with the splendid wild ones along the riverbank. A fence on the left guides up the path, which is an old track gradually sinking under the heather.

At the stony track above, turn left to ford a burn. After 200yds, turn right onto a wide forest road. Those who, earlier, decided to bypass Kinharvie, have been on this road all along. We are now on the 26 mile (40km) long-distance route from Criffel to Mabie. That walk is not waymarked, being intended for those who want to take on something more demanding than the conventional forest trail.

The forest road slants uphill to cross another branch of the Kinharvie Burn. At the 290m contour it turns sharply back left, and climbs to meet the former District Boundary at GR 918634. Just as the road starts to descend again, look for a small path below the road on the left. This runs along a ride, with the posts of the collapsed boundary fence first on the right, then on the left. It climbs through trees onto the open slopes of Meikle Hard Hill.

The path bends away from the fence, southeast, to follow the ridgeline towards Boreland Hill. It is reasonably distinct as it crosses heathery moorland. Isolated spruce trees, escaped from the plantation, are struggling to make a life outside the forest fence. On the final approach to Boreland Hill, a stone wall runs in from the left, once again marking the District Boundary (Nithsdale/Stewartry). The Forestry Commission route turns right alongside the wall, but we cross it through one of its gaps to the summit, which is marked by a cairn barely high enough to emerge from the heather.

Views southward over the Solway Firth are some compensation for the rough ground that follows. From Boreland Hill descend north-east into a broad col. A stone wall runs across the ridgeline. It can be climbed by a stone stile at its highest point. Briefly, new plantations approach the ridgeline, and the top-of-trees fence can be followed for a few steps. Continue straight uphill to a cairn at 550m altitude. A brief dip and climb lead to Criffel's summit trig.

The descent path starts from the cairn, not the trig point. In mist, it's easy to end on the wrong path now: after 50yds, where the path divides, take care to fork left (slightly west of north), as the path for Ardwall branches off. The correct path runs down the grassy basement of some peat hags, then contours along the wet eastern slopes of Criffel's northern spur. It bends right, to cross the small col to Knockendoch.

A clear path runs down northwards. At the 300m contour a forest-top wall runs in from the right to meet a forest-top fence running in from the left. Where they join, the fence is crossed by a stile. Go down to left of the wall. At the foot of the hill the path bends left to run into a forest road.

Follow the road downhill for 150yds. A path leads off left between gorse bushes. After 400yds this emerges at Mid Glen.

Walk 5:4
CRIFFEL from ARDWALL
$3^{1}/_{2}$ miles 1700ft ($5^{1}/_{2}$km 500m)
Steep rough path, pathless hill: moderate
See map with Walk 5:1 p105

This ascent is a relentless uphill pull from bottom to top. Those fit enough to cope will enjoy the bouldery wood of the lower part.

MAP: Landranger 84 (Dumfries)

Drive south from New Abbey for 2 miles (3km) and turn right onto a small farm road. There is parking space at a sign "Criffel Footpath".

START/FINISH: Ardwall farm (GR 971635)

❈ ❈ ❈

Turn left through the large metal gate indicated by the sign. After 100yds, a side track leads off to the right. This soon enters forest at a gate.

Now a forest track goes left, but keep ahead, uphill, on a small but clear path with a sign "Criffel". After 200yds, the path goes straight across a forest road, with another sign.

Below the larches, and even obstructing the path, appear the

SOLWAY COAST

speckled grey lumps of Criffel granite. This is one of Britain's most radioactive rocks; in southwest Scotland, only the Solway foreshore and the remains of Chernobyl fallout around Merrick have higher levels of radiation. These levels are not high, though they might trouble a hermit planning to dwell in caves of Criffel granite for long years.

At 200m the path crosses another forest road (not marked on the map). It continues up the strip of open ground to left of a stream. Fallen trunks mean a slight detour left into the plantation. There is an alternative path just inside the plantation, but the path beside the stream is more comfortable.

At the top of the trees, a stile leads out onto the open hill. The path continues on a straight line, slightly west of south, uphill to the summit of Criffel.

The path to Knockendoch starts from Douglas' Cairn, not the trig point, to cross the low remnant of a stone wall. 50yds from the summit it forks: beware, as it is easy to stray onto the branch that bends away down the eastern slopes to join our ascent route - so keep on the left-hand path. After descending the summit dome, the path contours around the east (right-hand) flank of Criffel's north ridge, then drops to right, into the small col leading to Knockendoch.

From Knockendoch's cairn descend south-east on fairly deep heather. A faint path is forming on the lower part of the descent, which is fairly steep. A stream runs down into the trees at the stile where the upward route is rejoined.

Walk 5:5
MABIE FOREST and MARTHROWN HILL
5 miles 1100ft (8km 350m)
Paths and tracks, but some pathless forest: easy + hard

The waymarked trails in Mabie are described in the following walk. However, the forest does contain a hill: the 249m (817ft) Marthrown. The quest for its hidden trig leads through the wild woods. Fallen trees, brushwood and boggy bits make up about a third of this walk.

The summit could be reached from the car park in about 40 minutes. That would be too straightforward. This walk tricks the hill into a false sense of security, setting off towards somewhere else and pretending

THE LOWTHER HILLS

to be interested only in the distant Lake District. We then creep round behind, to pounce suddenly from an unexpected direction.

MAP: Landranger 84 (Dumfries): A map of the five marked walks is obtainable from Forest Enterprise, Ae Village, Dumfries DG1 1QB (01387 86247)

START/FINISH: A signed turning off the A710 (Dumfries - New Abbey) leads to the Mabie Forest car park (GR 950709).

❋   ❋   ❋

Follow the brown waymarks (though this route appears on the map as the "Green Trail"). The waymarked trail crosses three forest roads before circling the side of Craigbill Hill for those views of the Lake District (more details, if required, in Walk 5:8 following). It joins a forest road to a T-junction.

Turn right, uphill. At the top of the hill is a junction with waymarks of a mountain bike trail, but just before this we turn off, left, on a faint rutted track marked as "path" on the FE map. After a few yards this is blocked by fallen trees; go round to the right, beside a small stream. After the obstruction the track continues uphill, on pine-needles, to left of the stream.

The track emerges into a felled area with a view ahead to

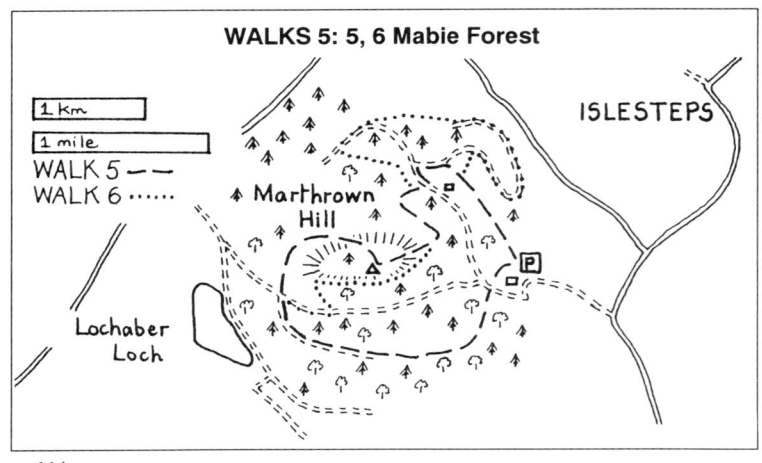

Dumfries. Bear right, with trees on the right, to cross a forest road after 100yds. Continue on a track that is faint, green, boggy and marked with wheel-ruts: cleared ground is on the left for the first 250yds, then the way enters trees, keeping always east. After another 300yds it becomes a pine-needle track climbing steeply to the right. This is marked with two yellow-top poles. At the second pole, turn off right to the trig point, which is 30yds away.

This is quite the mossiest trig point I've seen, and has a short view of trees. Head roughly southeast, continuing the arrival direction, through open wood to a ruined stone wall.

Newly-felled ground is beyond the wall, so turn left along it, through some fallen trees and difficult going. Soon the wall turns downhill, through easier open woodland. Follow it down: a track forms alongside, and the White Trail joins for the last few yards down to a forest road.

The White Trail's waymarks lead along the road to the left for 400yds, then right, along a green ride, to Marthrown of Mabie outdoor centre. Turn left along the forest road, passing through a gate to a track junction. Here the White Trail continues on forest road, but leave it to turn down right on an earth path that joins a stream.

The White Trail rejoins from the left, to continue downstream on a track. The path turns off left to a footbridge. Waymarks, increasingly multi-coloured, lead to the sawmill, and to the long footbridge over the Mabie Burn. The car park is just above.

Walk 5:6
MABIE FOREST WALKS
1-7 miles (2-11km)
Waymarked paths: easy
See map with Walk 5:5

It was during the First World War that a strategic shortage of pit-props led to the setting up of the Forestry Commission. The first hillsides disappeared under the Sitka Spruce: but the spruce was barely big enough for Christmas trees by the time pit-props started to be made of steel not timber.

The most recent approach to forestry, known blandly as "Restructuring", intends that each tree should have as many purposes as possible. It should eventually be turned into rafters or chipboard, but until then should be a bird reserve, or a nice place for people. At the back of Criffel (Walk 5:3) money is the main motive, though even there the edges of the plantations are being made ragged, hillsides felled in smaller swathes, and birch and rowan planted here and there.

Here at Mabie, the Forestry Commission aims to persuade us that the tree is the place to be. Beech, oak, sycamore, larch are mixed in with the commercial evergreens. Paths have been laid, and an adventure playground. Trees have been felled to provide viewpoints. At weekends the forest is busy with cyclists and orienteers as well as walkers.

In spring when the leaves are breaking, or during the autumn colours, a walk in the woods can be as good as a walk on the hills. And when the clouds are down, the wind is up, and the rain is falling sideways, the walk in the woods is a whole lot better.

The shortest walk (red) is 1 mile (1½km) and suitable for wheelchairs - though if there's such a thing as an "all-terrain wheelchair", that'd be the one to use. The longest walk is summarised below. There are also mountain bike trails, and bikes can be hired.

The Longest MABIE TRAIL
7 miles 11km
Clear, well-waymarked paths and tracks: easy

MAP of the five marked walks is obtainable from Forest Enterprise, Ae Village, Dumfries DG1 1QB (01387 86247)

START/FINISH: A signed turning off the A710 (Dumfries - New Abbey) leads to the Mabie Forest car park (GR 950709).

✳ ✳ ✳

Descend from the car park following multicoloured waymarks, and turn off left, before the long footbridge, onto the Brown Trail (marked as the Green Trail on the FE map). This doubles back left across a small stream, and climbs through oaks to cross two forest roads.

After the second road, the Brown Trail continues alone, the White and the Yellow having turned off along the road. It passes along to right of open ground, crosses a third road, and traverses around the back of Craigbill Hill. Steep slopes below are clothed in

SOLWAY COAST

granite boulders and aged oak, and there's a view out to Criffel, the Solway, and the English hills.

The path bends down left, to join a forest road and continue around the hillside, above Lochaber Loch, to a T-junction. Turn right, on a main forest road that climbs to a pass and then descends beside a stream. After descending for $^{1}/_{2}$ mile ($^{3}/_{4}$km), watch out for the White Trail crossing. Bend sharply back left, uphill.

The White Trail soon doubles back right, to cross a steep slope above cliffs, with fine outlooks. It drops to a forest road and follows this to the left. After $^{1}/_{4}$ mile ($^{1}/_{2}$km) it turns off right on a wide grassy ride, to reach the outdoor centre of Marthrown of Mabie. Above the houses, the waymarked Yellow Trail turns up to the left.

The Yellow Trail follows a green ride, crossing one forest road and turning right on the second. It circles the northern side of the aptly named Larch Hill, with outlooks towards Dumfries and Queensberry. Turn down left on a wide path waymarked in blue, white and yellow.

A broad track leads down to right of a stream, then a path turns off left across a footbridge. After $^{1}/_{4}$ mile ($^{1}/_{2}$km) under tall beeches, turn right, crossing the stream again, to the sawmill buildings in their wide clearing. Beyond them is the long footbridge leading back up to the car park.

Walk 5:7
** SANDYHILLS COAST (SANDYHILLS to ROCKCLIFFE)
$8^{1}/_{2}$ miles 1400ft ($13^{1}/_{2}$km 400m) for the return journey
Well-marked path, quite steep in places, occasionally muddy: easy

---

This is a very attractive coastal walk, with interesting rock-scenery and views to nearby islands and distant English hills. The route is frequented by cows, and crosses fairly steep slopes. Gorse encroaches at some points, to the discomfort of those with bare legs.

VARIANTS: The very best way to do this walk is with a car at either end. However, it will often be more convenient to return to Sandyhills on foot. The return along the narrow and busy A710 is not advised. The return by the same route is one good idea: this walk is quite good enough to do both out and back. Alternatively, a route may be made through the Dalbeattie forest. This is described at the end of the walk.

THE LOWTHER HILLS

MAP: Landranger 84 (Dumfries)
START: Sandyhills beach car park (GR 891552)
FINISH: Rockcliffe: no parking along sea front, but large car park at entrance to the village (GR 852536).

✳   ✳   ✳

From Sandyhills, a wooden path from the corner of the car park leads onto the beach. Turn right along the sand, to find the beginning of the path after 200yds. Cross grass to a footbridge over a stream.

After the bridge the path divides; take the right fork, up through trees, to a signpost and gate. Here the main path continues uphill to a kissing-gate. (It is possible, if the tide is low, to bear left here onto the sand and mud of the foreshore. Walk below cliffs to the Needle's Eye, a fine natural arch. You can then continue along the foreshore to Portling. However, the time of low tide should be checked first. The Mersehead sands are flat, and the incoming tide arrives suddenly. It is possible to become trapped against the cliffs.)

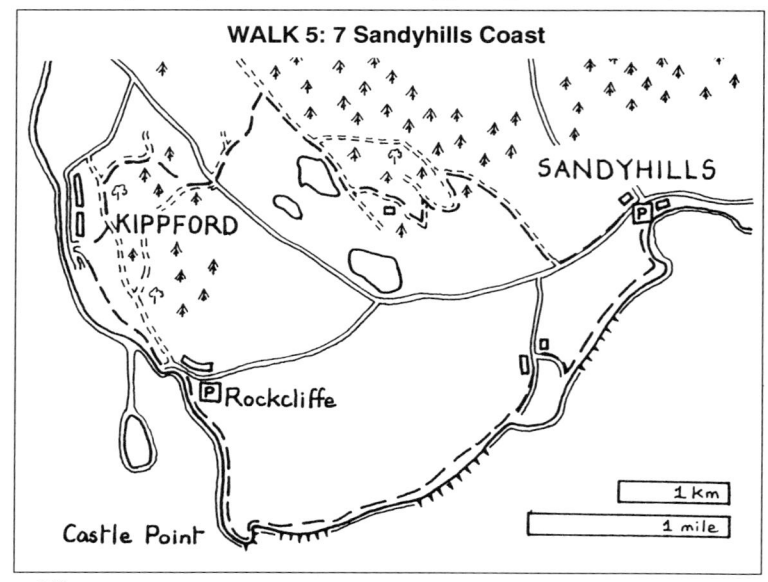

WALK 5: 7 Sandyhills Coast

SOLWAY COAST

After the kissing-gate the path continues along field edges next to the clifftop, with views forward and down to the Needle's Eye, and to the stake-nets spread for salmon across the muddy flats below. It climbs steeply up wood-faced steps, to a viewpoint table, then crosses along the tops of considerable cliffs. The way then drops gradually to the lane end at Portling.

Signs point the way through the village: turn right, uphill, then left on a tarred lane with cottages. This becomes unsurfaced as it drops towards Port o' Warren. At the start of the village, turn right at a signpost across a stone stile. The path climbs steeply through gorse to cross the flank of White Hill. It continues beside the final field-edge next to the sea, with stiles where it crosses granite field walls. After a mile (1 1/2km), you can drop left to a conical concrete cairn below the path, set among grass-topped rocks. This commemorates the providential landing of the crew of the schooner *Elbe*, who scrambled ashore here from their sinking ship.

The path passes the heads of deep inlets carved into the rock. At a ruined cottage, the beach below is completely enclosed, the sea being out of sight down two twisting channels. The path rises again above cliffs along the side of Barcloy Hill; at low tide, a way can be made along the beach below. The two routes converge at the headland of Castle Point: an ancient fort with a modern viewpoint table mounted on it.

Continue along the field edge for 200yds. The path turns off left to thread its way between rocks. It passes through scrubby woodland or along the pebbly foreshore to the end of the lane that leads into Rockcliffe.

Rockcliffe is a pretty village with a small sandy beach. The car park is up right, at the edge of the village. Alternatively, enjoy an ice cream before returning by the same route.

* CONTINUATION to KIPPFORD, with ALTERNATIVE RETURN by DALBEATTIE FOREST
10 miles 1000ft (16km 300m) for the complete circuit

Paths, occasionally muddy: easy
Attractive coastal walking continues for another mile to Kippford, where a second ice cream can be enjoyed. The return journey through the trees is not as impressive as the shore path, but it is shorter and more

THE LOWTHER HILLS

sheltered, and it is attractive in its own right. Scrub birch and oak, ancient pines and a stretch of water combine to make this more genuine than most of the artificial plantations that claim the name of forest. The forest roads have declined and shrunk into narrow paths between the encroaching trees.

Parking at the entrance to Rockcliffe, and at Sandyhills beach. Also parking and shop at Kippford.

START/FINISH: Sandyhills, Rockcliffe or Kippford

✻ ✻ ✻

From Rockcliffe to Kippford there is a selection of paths, detailed on a map at the end of Rockcliffe's beach. The route described here combines shoreline and woodland, but a lower route allows a crossing of the causeway to Rough Island (see note at the end of the walk description).

At the end of the tarred road is a toilet block and the signboard with the path map. Continue past these for a few yards, and turn right at a sign for Mote of Mark. Before you reach cottages, another sign points right through two kissing-gates.

In the field beyond, a waymark points forward, but instead keep left along the bottom edge of the field to a plank bridge and a rough track leading to more cottages. Just before these, turn right onto a path. This runs below a small crag, then along through trees above the water (or above the mud, if the tide is out).

As the path starts to climb, it forks. Take the left fork, under power lines, for 50yds, then turn up right, to pass between two benches onto the well-made Jubilee Path. Follow this to the left, through woods, till it ends at the top of a street leading down into Kippford.

Kippford

Follow the shoreline road for a few yards. Turn up opposite the slipway on an unsurfaced lane that passes the lifeboat station. The lane bends left, becoming tarred, and here a path ahead climbs steeply through a wood of oaks to a forest track.

These tracks are not used by vehicles, and are narrow and grassy.

Turn left along the first track, ignoring the first turning on the right (signed "Rockcliffe"), and the second (a dead end), to cross the end of Mark Hill and descend slightly to a crossroads. (Mark Hill is the unnamed 100m contour ring on Landranger, while the hill there named as "Mark Hill" is in fact Muckle Hill.)

Fifty yards along the left-hand track is a small pond lost among the trees: our way, though, goes ahead, on a stony track that descends and then rises to a left bend. Here turn off right, onto a small path running just south of east through the trees. After $^{1}/_{4}$ mile ($^{1}/_{2}$km) it emerges onto a well-used track. Turn left, to reach the A710 at Rock Cottage, near the Clonyard Hotel.

Cross left, into a tarred lane. Where this branches, keep right for Auchensheen. Go round to left of this house through two gates, following a sign "Access to Forest". Follow a wall on the right, on traces of an old stony track, to enter the trees at a gate. The path runs up to a forest road: turn right, signed "Colvend".

The track passes Barean Loch: a beautiful stretch of water with lilies, and a small island that is the remains of a 'crannog' or lake village. At the loch's end a grassy track running ahead is the way to Colvend, but our route turns up left on the main track, to reach the abandoned house of Smithland after $^{1}/_{4}$ mile ($^{1}/_{2}$km).

A track on the right leads towards the house, and opposite it a path leads up left into the trees. This is fairly clear, used by horses. It bends left to avoid a swampy bit, and then turns sharply right: a sign "horses" points back towards us at this point. The path is here the barely discernible line of a forgotten forest road, and has firm dry footing; it heads just south of east, to run alongside a small stream or ditch.

At a T-junction, turn up left on a clearer track, climbing gently for $^{1}/_{4}$ mile ($^{1}/_{2}$km) along a wide ride with encroaching bracken. Take the first side-track, sharply back right, descending. It leads to a gate out of the forest onto a well-used driveway track.

Keep ahead, over a cattle grid, to reach the A710. Turn left along this fairly busy road, which is narrow with some blind corners but does have a reasonable verge to walk on. After $^{3}/_{4}$ mile (1km) it leads into Sandyhills.

Rough Island

Rough Island, in the middle of the estuary opposite Rockcliffe, can

THE LOWTHER HILLS

be reached by a stony causeway. It is well worth visiting. There are, however, three warnings. The island is a bird sanctuary, and is closed to humans during the nesting season April to June. The causeway is covered at high tide. And, because it is so covered, its stones are well mixed with mud: suitable footwear is wellingtons, or nothing at all.

Walk 5:8
** SCREEL alone
3 miles 1200ft (4$^{1}/_{2}$km 400m)
Path, steep and rocky in places: easy/moderate
SCREEL HILL with BENGAIRN
5 miles 1800ft (8km 550m)
moderate/hard

With Bengairn and Screel both below 400m, few will concern themselves as to which of the two is the bigger. The better of the two is Screel. This small hill has enough rock sticking out of it to do for a middle-sized mountain. A well-laid path through the forest makes a peaceful introduction to a steep final ascent. The short half-mile of summit ridge has rocks on, and a view back over Auchencairn Bay. And if the hill sounds familiar, that may be because, in the Gaelic spelling, it's Sgritheall (scree hill); the Galloway Screel is not altogether unworthy of its namesake above Loch Hourn in the far north.

Screel alone is a fine walk, and the out-and-back to Bengairn can certainly be omitted. The extra ground consists of bog path under branches, and rough moorland. The reward for the extra effort is a top that's higher than Screel, and also quieter, while being very nearly as rocky. Interestingly, it's a different sort of rock.

MAP: Landranger 84 (Dumfries)

Turn off the A711 onto the second minor road to Gelston. The Forest Enterprise car park is on the left after 300yds.

START/FINISH: Screel car park (GR 800547)

✻ ✻ ✻

At quiet times, the walk can be started by taking the mountain bike trail uphill straight out of the car park, and turning left at the forest

SOLWAY COAST

WALK 5: 8 Screel Hill and Bengairn

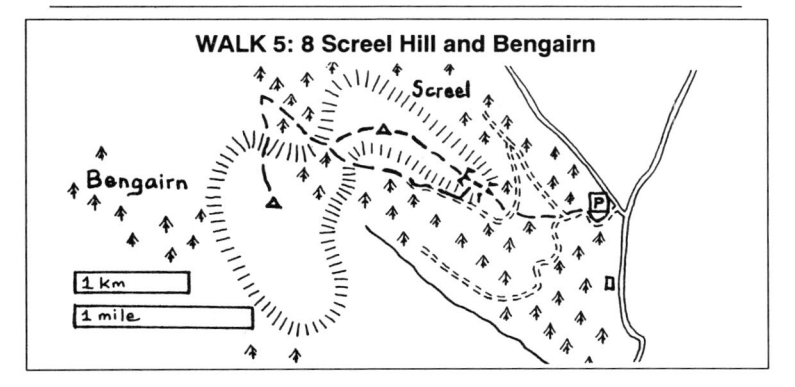

road above for 300yds to a junction. If the cyclists are using their trail, then take the forest road out of the car park to the same junction.

A path marked with white-banded waymarks leads up into the trees. It isn't all that clear over the pine-needles, and a sharp eye needs to be kept for the waymarks. Go straight across another forest road and continue uphill to the top of the trees.

Above the treeline, a direct path may be taken through the rocks above. However, the waymarked path slants across left onto the southern flank of the hill, then turns sharply back right: at this turning a lesser path, to be ignored, continues ahead. Either way, a sharp climb brings you onto the eastern top of Screel. A clear path, muddy in places, rocky in others, winds its way in and out, up and down, to the main summit with its large cairn.

Descend steeply westward for a short distance over heather and bare rock. The path enters forest alongside a broken wall. After 50yds it turns off left into a narrow track with pine-needle floor: here the extension to Bengairn will continue ahead.

The pine-needle path goes downhill for 3/4 mile (1km), to reach the end of a forest road directly under the east summit of Screel. You can continue along this road for another 3/4 mile of gentle downhill to rejoin the upward route: keep a sharp eye open for the white-topped waymark where the path crosses the track. Alternatively, for a more exciting finish:

Where the path meets the road end, turn uphill for 40yds up a

THE LOWTHER HILLS

waterlogged ride, to emerge from the trees at the foot of the steep flank of Screel. A small path zigzags upwards, crossing bare rock here and there. The slope eases slightly after 100ft (30m vertical), and now the path slants up right, then traverses. It joins the waymarked ascent route at its sharp bend. Follow the path as it slants down to the top of the trees, for a rapid pine-needle descent to the car park.

EXTENSION to BENGAIRN

After the descent from Screel, where the track turns off left, the small path for Bengairn continues ahead beside the wall. This path is being encroached on by branches: bring your clippers and earn a blessing from future walkers. The path climbs briefly, then descends to emerge from the trees alongside the Linkins Burn (GR 770553). Cross the short section of fence where the wall meets the stream.

Turn left, uphill, alongside the stone wall and the edge of the forest. After 200yds, strike uphill slantwise, hoping to find the small path that heads directly for the summit of Bengairn. A trig point and two cairns decorate the summit.

Bengairn is the western corner of the Criffel granite: a lump of underground molten magma forced its way up into the older shales and mudstones. Screel is some hundred million years older than Bengairn. As the direct descent from Bengairn involves bracken and barbed wire, the return is by the outward route. This lets you search the Linkins Burn for the transition between the Bengairn granite and the Screel shale.

At the base of Screel's steep end, turn right onto the waymarked pine-needle path and continue as on the shorter walk.

Walk 5:9
* BALCARY POINT WALKS
1¹/₂ miles (2¹/₂ km), with longer alternatives up to
6 miles 500ft (10km 150m)
Waymarked paths, but including a section of exposed clifftop: moderate

---

The 1¹/₂ mile short circuit of Balcary Point is the shortest walk in this book; it can also claim to be the most exciting. Below the path, sheer cliffs of 200ft (50m) plunge into the Solway Firth. And if the Solway fog obscures the views of the Lake District hills, there are weird rock-formations beside the path to take photos of. For those who want to walk a bit further, the extension to Castle Muir Point is less spectacular but still worthwhile, with a peaceful return journey by forest, field and fishing-loch.

MAP: Landranger 84 (Dumfries)

From Auchencairn take the small scenic road to the Balcary Hotel. At the hotel entrance keep right.

START/FINISH: Car park behind Balcary Hotel (GR 821495)

✳   ✳   ✳

SHORT WALK: BALCARY POINT only
$1^1/_2$ miles ($2^1/_2$km)

Ignore the "right-of-way" signpost pointing west, and follow the road south for 20yds to a sharp bend left. Here walk ahead around the end of a gate, following footpath signs for Balcary Point and Rascarrel. After a few yards a footpath sign points right "alternative route, Rascarrel": ignore this, which is the return route of the shortest walk. Instead go ahead through a kissing gate signed "Balcary Point and Rascarrel".

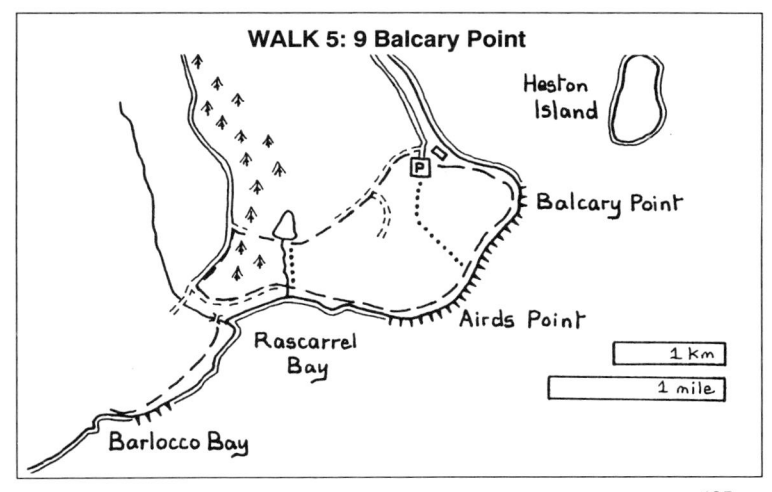

The field ahead has no visible path. Walk round its left-hand edge, with trees below on the left and sea below the trees. At the far corner a kissing-gate opens onto a broad path through the woods. The woods end after 300yds at a hidden stone boathouse. Here the path divides: the lower branch winds awkwardly through gorse, the upper is by the field edge, but they soon rejoin. At Balcary Point, fallen boulders form natural arches across a deep sea inlet.

Now the path turns south-west to climb above the high cliffs. Notices warn of danger, and that walkers proceed at our own risk. The path, though narrow, is a few feet upslope from the serious drops. As it descends, you look down on the gull-covered pinnacle of Lot's Wife. At the lowest point of the path is a kissing-gate of tubular steel overhanging the void. (HERE THE LONGER ROUTES CONTINUE AHEAD.)

Go through the kissing-gate, and back through a field gate alongside. Walk inland, with a wall on your left, to a field gate. This leads onto a stony track which is followed for just 50yds to a waymark. Bear off slightly right across a field to a waymark at the hedge corner below. Follow the grassy track to the right alongside the hedge. It reaches a gate that is falling off its hinges and should be lifted aside with care. The track continues between hedges to rejoin the outward route south of the car park.

BALCARY POINT to BARLOCCO
6 miles 500ft (10km 150m)

Start as on the short route. From the kissing-gate at Lot's Wife, a good path leads on along the clifftops with a wall alongside. Airds Point is marked by a wooden cross-like structure which presumably assists seamen. The rock is a pinkish conglomerate, a sort of Christmas pudding. Even the pebbles embedded in it are younger than any of the surrounding rocks of Galloway.

After another $^{1}/_{4}$ mile ($^{1}/_{2}$km) of clifftop, the path descends to the shore, and passes along the base of low bluffs. At the corner of Rascarrel Bay the path divides in front of some gaily-painted beach shacks. (Pass to right of these shacks for a shorter route home. After a kissing gate the path becomes a tractor track to right of a plantation, and joins the homeward route at a signpost beside Loch Markie.)

Pass to left of the beach shacks. A sandy track leads along the

Sea stacks at Airds Point

foreshore of Rascarrel Bay to a footbridge over the Tachar Burn. Here is a small car park. Cross the footbridge and take the path either above or along the front of some more beach huts. It continues along the low clifftops to Castle Muir Point, where those with bare legs will be turned back by low-growing gorse. Barlocco Bay, just beyond, offers a sand-and-shingle beach with real remoteness, though the tideline seems to attract more than its share of plastic debris.

Return to Rascarrel, and after recrossing the footbridge, turn inland along a sandy lane to a minor road. Turn right for $^1/_2$ mile ($^3/_4$km) to a signposted track on the right, "Loch Markie $^1/_2$". The track leads into forest; where it ends, the footpath starts between two green signs asking us to keep to the footpath. It winds its way pleasantly between larches to Loch Markie. To save those without their glasses from a peaty swim, I reveal that the notice in the middle of the water says "Private Fishing".

At the signpost beside Loch Markie continue east, to left of a wall, on grassy ruts. At the first gate this becomes a rough track. After Airds Cottage, the entrance track of Airds farm joins from the right. Continue ahead to the car park.

Cairnsmore summit cairn, sunset, Cree estuary (Walks 6:1, 6:2, 6:3)
Cairn on the granite plateau near Craignelder (Walk 6:3)

The cairn on Cairn Table (Walk 7:1)
Tinto from the east, with Pap Craig (Walk 7:3)

6: Cairnsmore of Fleet

Cairnsmore of Fleet is a great granite lump - not the highest, but perhaps the wildest hill in Galloway. Right beside the sea, and the southernmost hill in Scotland, it gets the weather before anywhere else. The result is a high-altitude, high-rainfall bog of international importance. This doesn't make for easy walking.

The usual route comes straight up from Cairnsmore farm (Walk 6:1). It's a well-built, straightforward path. It misses out much of the difficulty, and much of the interest too. The international bog, with

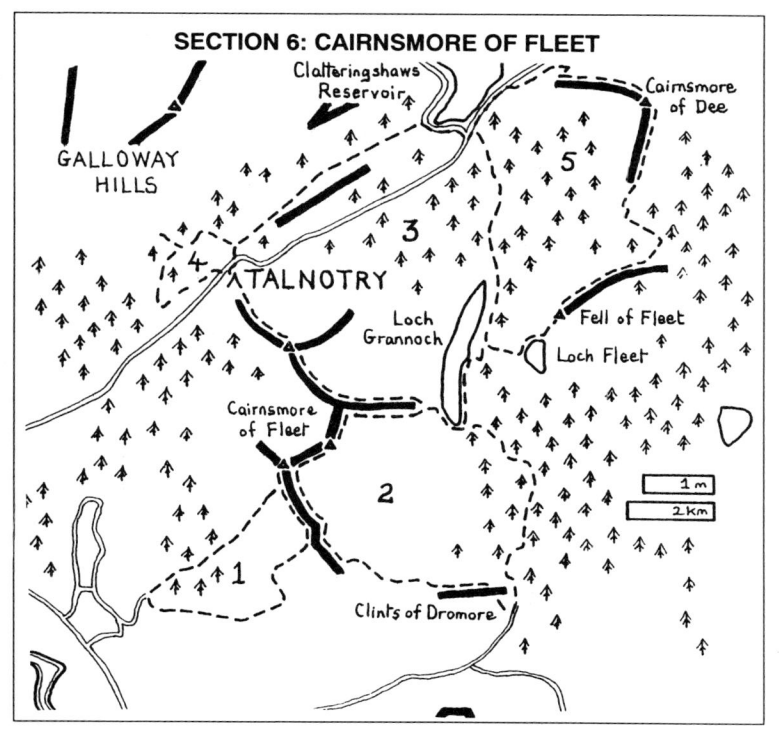

THE LOWTHER HILLS

its black peat and bare silver slabs, lies away to the north, on the route from Talnotry (Walk 6:3). The wild and granity crags lie on the eastern flank, and this aspect of the mountain is appreciated on Walk 6:2 from the Visitor Centre near Gatehouse Station.

Proximity alone has put the Whithorn coast walk into this section. Walk 6:6 is a grassy stroll along a low but rocky coastline, accompanied by rabbits, the swishing of the sea, and pious memories of St Ninian.

Walk 6:1
CAIRNSMORE OF FLEET from CAIRNSMORE FARM
* STRAIGHT-UP-AND-DOWN
6 miles 2200ft (9½km 650m)
Path: moderate/easy going, but in serious hilltop surroundings
** DESCENT by KNEE OF CAIRNSMORE
8 miles 2300ft (12km 700m)
Path, easy moor, track, but a rough rocky descent: moderate/hard

The shortest route from car park to summit, and back down, is rarely the best way, and it's not the best way on Cairnsmore. However, it is the easiest way; the other, better, routes involve rough pathless ground with boulders. And Cairnsmore is such a fine mountain that even the short route is quite nice enough to deserve your walking up it.

The longer variant turns Walk 6:1 into another of the tough routes. The initial drop off Knee of Cairnsmore involves heather and granite boulderfield, and navigational error could lead onto the crags of Door of Cairnsmore.

However, the inclusion of the extra top allows some plateau-walking, with views into the rocky interior of the massif; and the finish, by the Graddoch track, is easy and enjoyable. This is altogether a better route than the straight-up-and-down.

MAP: Landranger 83 (Newton Stewart) or OL 32 (Galloway)

Turn off the A75 at Muirfad, and take the track marked "Cairnsmore Estate" between the arches of an abandoned railway viaduct. This runs up through beechwoods beside the Cairnsmore Burn. The track reaches the former stable-block, white-painted with a handsome granite arch. Drive round to left of this, to a T-junction above. A few yards left is a small car park under trees.

CAIRNSMORE OF FLEET

If the car park is full, there is verge parking between the A75 and the viaduct. This adds nearly a mile to each end of the walk: but a nice mile.

START/FINISH: Cairnsmore farm (GR 471640)

✻ ✻ ✻

Just past the car park is a grey gate leading into a field. Slant up this to a gate and stile in its top left corner. A clear path leads up through the trees. It crosses a forest road at the 200m contour, and continues to a ladderstile at the top of the trees.

It carries on in well-graded zigzags. It levels onto the summit plateau: this is the only boggy bit of the route. The plateau becomes stony, and the path is marked with small cairns for the final 400yds to the summit.

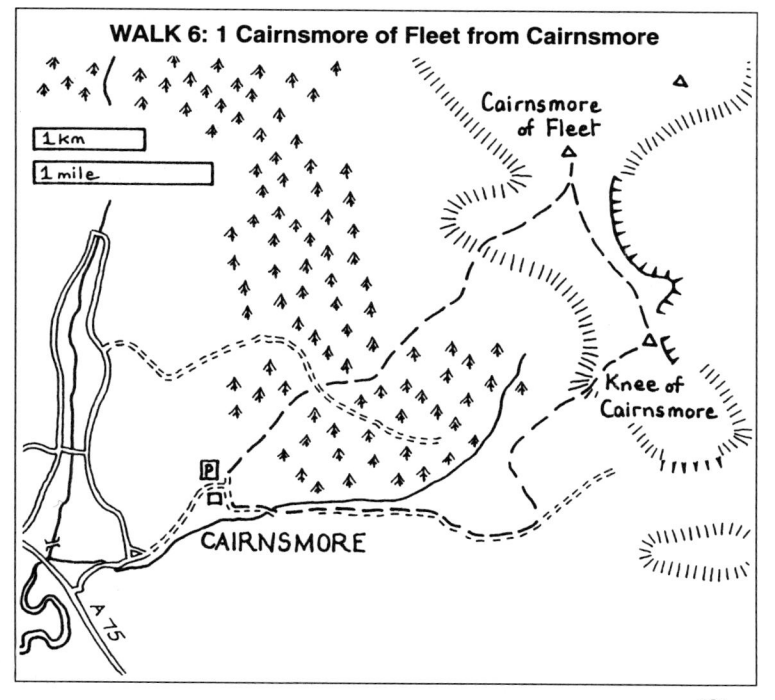

WALK 6: 1 Cairnsmore of Fleet from Cairnsmore

THE LOWTHER HILLS

The cairns along this path are fully justified. The summit plateau is confusing in mist, and the path marked is the safe way off. This said, there is no requirement for the cairns to be enlarged. It is instructive to compare these ancient and useful cairns with those that proliferate on more popular ranges; the latter being constructed for purposes of personal self-assertion as much as anything. The cairns on the Cairnsmore are small - no more than 2ft (80cm) high - and closely spaced, at around 10yds apart. Where pathside cairns are desirable at all, this is the sort of cairns they should be.

The top is marked by a large Bronze Age cairn, a trig point, and the ruins of a small hut. There is also a granite slab commemorating the crews of eight aircraft that came to grief on Cairnsmore.

The shorter route descends by the same way. From the airmen's memorial, the initial direction is south, to find the first cairns of the path.

DESCENT by KNEE OF CAIRNSMORE

From the summit, go back along the cairned path for 200yds, then branch off left, just east of south, rising very slightly across the grassy plateau. The posts of a ruined fence guide down into the col called Nick of Clashneach.

Here a wall crosses. Go through a gap, and up the slope of rocks and grass. There is no path, and the large cairn of Knee is no longer in sight. In mist, this is confusing ground: at the top of the slope, you must turn half-right, south, to find the cairn at the far end of the plateau.

From the cairn descend southwest, aiming towards the distant point where the Cree meets the sea. Most of the descent is on rough grass, but then it steepens and becomes heather and boulder: slow and difficult ground.

At the foot of the slope (300m contour) the ground changes again. We are now on moor of cropped grass and heather, pleasant and easy walking. Turn left (south), crossing the trickle of the Torr Burn, to find the green path on Knocktim. The OS maps have this as a track, but it is merely a wide path, though with signs of having been something grander in past centuries.

At the wall corner below Knocktim, the path becomes a vehicle track, and descends beside the Torr Burn to join the Graddoch Burn.

Here is a small gorge below high pines. At a field-top gate the track vanishes. Go down the field, with wall on right, to find the track again at the bottom corner of the field. It goes down between rhododendrons, crosses the stream, and returns you to the car park at Cairnsmore farm.

Walk 6:2
* CAIRNSMORE and THE CLINTS from DROMORE
12 miles 3100ft (19km 950m)
Bog, rough hillside and rocks: hard

From the low ground of the coast, Cairnsmore appears as a broad hump of a hill. Its wild romantic side is revealed only on this approach from the southeast. Here is country of heather and boulder, of wild goats and eagles. The walk is largely pathless, and one of the toughest in this book. Only the 3 miles (4½km) through the forest prevents it from gaining the top grade of **.

Just west of the bridge in Gatehouse, take the small road northwards signed "Cairnsmore of Fleet Nature Reserve". After 5 miles (8km), at a wild moorland T-junction, turn right. Car parking is at the Visitor Centre in 1 mile (1½km).

MAP: Landranger 83 (Newton Stewart) or OL 32 (Galloway)
START/FINISH: Visitor Centre, Dromore farm (GR 554637)

❊ ❊ ❊

I'm not keen on Visitor Attractions like the Mill of the Fleet in Gatehouse, but this one at Dromore I do like. It's small; it's free; and instead of video screens it has plaster relief models of the mountain. Take the track northeast to pass under the viaduct - this structure is no longer used by trains, but for training: youngsters from Loch Grannoch Lodge have practised abseiling off it.

The track continues northwards, to enter the forest. After ¼ mile (½km) turn right, and soon afterwards go straight across the double T-junction near Meikle Cullendoch. All these turnings are signed "Loch Grannoch Lodge". After 400yds bear left, and after another long mile (2km) turn left again. These track junctions too are signposted for the Lodge.

THE LOWTHER HILLS

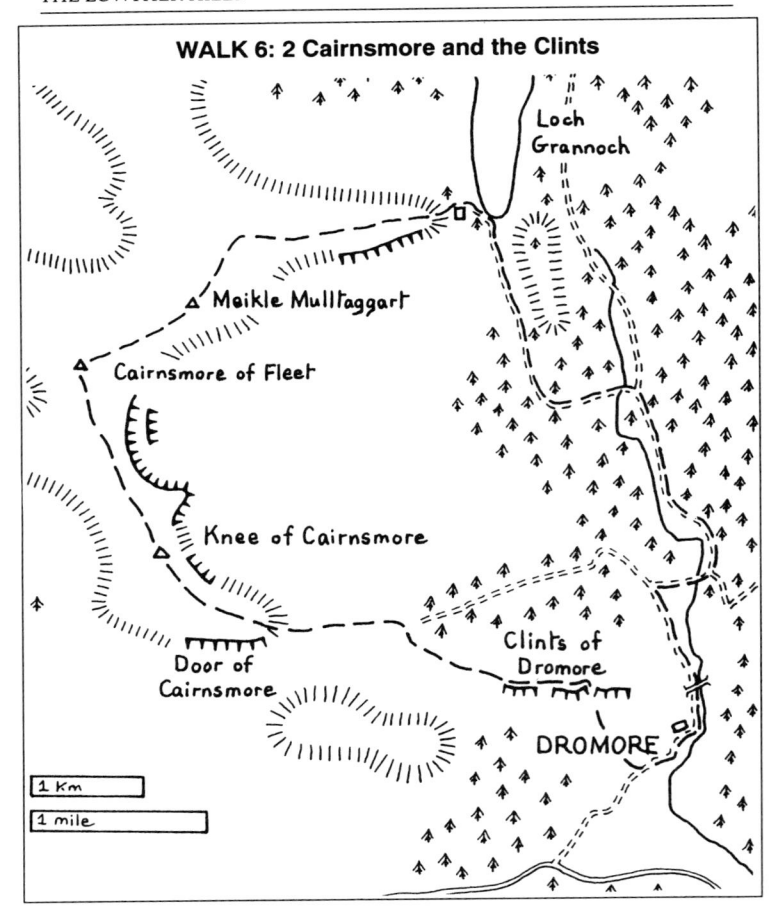

WALK 6: 2 Cairnsmore and the Clints

At the low but rocky little pass of Cleuch of Eglon, Loch Grannoch appears before you. At the pass itself a small memorial is dedicated "to Maggie": clearly a dear companion of the hill, and whether human or dog is not our concern. The track drops to the head of the loch, and passes into the attractive wood of rhododendron

Fence leads down from the summit of Cairnsmore of Fleet

and pine that shelters the Lodge. The Lodge itself is used as an outdoor centre.

Turn up past the Lodge, and take a path along the front of a small stone shed above, to the stream and small waterfall that lead to the top of the wood. The spur of Craigronald ahead is craggy on the left-hand (south) side, but merely broken ground on the right. Near the bottom and slightly left of centre appears a slab with a crackline slanting up leftwards. The crackline has good holds, especially to start with, and becomes quite exposed. Having crossed the slab, you are well positioned on the left flank for further scrambling. To avoid all scrambling, keep to right of the slab, and go up the crest of the nose. Any rock difficulties can be avoided by a detour to the right.

Above the steep section, the going is easy on short heather between scattered boulders. The cairn on Craigronald is a fine viewpoint to the higher summits of Cairnsmore, and a goat path leads onwards along the ridge. The ridge meets the main mountain at a cairn (GR 516687): just before this is a fence, which is crossed by a complicated stile structure. From the cairn the going is grassy. It's 400yds on 240° to the unnamed and unmarked summit of 585m - the

THE LOWTHER HILLS

name of it is, in fact, Millfore.

The going continues grassy and pleasant on the slight drop to a col and the gentle climb to Meikle Mulltaggart. This summit has neither cairn nor path. In mist, compass-bearings will be required to find the col before Cairnsmore. In this col is a three-way meeting of fences, with stiles: go uphill, beside, and to the right of, the southward fence. As this fence wanders away to the left, forge uphill on grassy slopes. The summit structures are various: trig pillar, the remains of a small hut, Bronze Age cairn and memorial to fallen airmen.

The broad flat ridge continues southeastwards. The cairned path can be followed for a few yards, but soon it veers off right. Follow the broad plateau as it bends round southeastward. Tops of large cliffs on the left, and a line of collapsing fence posts, mark the descent to the col, where you pass through the remains of a stone wall. A bouldery slope leads to the summit cairn of Knee of Cairnsmore. This cairn is another fine Bronze Age pile, with views along the Cree estuary to the open sea.

From Knee the main ridgeline descends southeast. Followed uncritically, this leads to the brink of the crags at Door of Cairnsmore. If this is the Door, it's better to leave by the window; the granite slabs are smooth, greasy and covered in poorly-attached plant life. So, having descended some 500ft (150m vertical), veer round eastward (left).

Drop down steepish heather, to join a new fence for the final descent to the boggy flats around the Cardoon Burn. Just beyond the southern branch of the burn (GR 525646), the wheelmarks of a quad bike may be found - these are easier to see from above than they are once you're right down beside them. Found, they lead east to where a track emerges from forest at a wooden gate (GR 532646).

The weary can follow this track down through the trees to rejoin the outward route 1/2 mile (3/4km) north of the viaduct. The less weary turn up the edge of the forest, and follow a fence to the ridgeline just west (right) of the Clints of Dromore. Turn left along the tops of the granite lumps that are the Clints.

The Clints alternate bare rock and tiring heather; the most amusing route passes over as much rock as possible. A few short scrambles are possible on sound rock, but all can be walked round. Views backwards are to the interesting flank of Cairnsmore.

After crossing half the Clints, a steep little dividing valley (Deep Nick of Dromore) holds a small pool. The climb out of the Nick, taken direct, offers a short scramble onto the highest Clint. Walk down the backslope of this Clint to find a bouldery open gully on the right, leading down onto the moor. (Or cross one more Clint, for a slightly more demanding descent to the foot of the same open gully.) Pass through a wooden fence-gate, and cross damp pastures to join the line of the former railway at the point where it emerges from the forest and crosses the Russon Burn. A wide gate leads onto the rough track along the railbed.

Cross the railbed to a smaller gate. This opens onto a waymarked path that leads down by way of a long stretch of duckboarding to join the tarred access track of Dromore. Turn left for 300yds to the Visitor Centre.

Walk 6:3
* CAIRNSMORE OF FLEET from TALNOTRY
16¹/₂ miles 2900ft (27km 900m)
Rough bogs and rocks, with 4 miles of forest road and an easier path to finish: hard

Cairnsmore of Fleet is a grand granite lump, and the grandest side of it, the lumpiest and the most granity, is the north slope overlooking Talnotry campsite. This long circuit gives you a stiff dose of lumps and heather, and then the full crossing of the plateau past the Coo Lochans, which is the same stuff laid flat and the gaps filled with water and black peat.

As well as all that, you get a descent that's just as steep and rocky, a mile of boggy lochside, and a long walk home along the Old Edinburgh Road. Scotland's sad Queen Mary, who used this route on pilgrimage to Whithorn (Walk 6.6), would have been a lot sadder if she'd been compelled to go up Cairnsmore as well...

The walk can also be taken in reverse, offering some scrambling up the face of Craig Ronald; care must be taken descending off Craignelder to find the gap with stone wall running through the trees. In this direction it will be best to start and finish at the track end beside Clatteringshaws dam (to allow a roadwalk finish for those who run out of daylight).

MAP: OL 32 (Galloway) or Landrangers 77 (Dalmellington) and 83 (Newton Stewart)

THE LOWTHER HILLS

START/FINISH: Grey Mare's Tail car park, immediately east of Talnotry Campsite (GR 491720)

✻   ✻   ✻

Turn into the campsite. From the campsite shop follow the track to the river, where are stepping stones. A small path leads through bog myrtle to join a stone wall that runs up through a gap in the trees onto the open hill. Go straight up, with the steep rock-slope of Big Gairy on the right. As the ridge becomes less steep, bare rock allows you to get out of the heather-and-peat. In mist, note that while preliminary knolls are cairned, the actual top of Craignelder has three small cairns, none actually at the highest point.

The summit of Millfore, a single metre higher, is $^{1}/_{4}$ mile ($^{1}/_{2}$km) away northeast, but could be omitted in mist as it makes the subsequent aiming-off along the flat plateau much more difficult.

Descend into the flat but rocky ground leading to the Coo Lochans: a fence runs across the plateau, and has a stile at its highest point, which is on the direct line to the lochans. Cross more stone and bog to gain the grassy slope of the 587m top beyond. This is also called 'Millfore', but not named on the OS map. Skirt its western slope into the col beyond, and go up to the unmarked summit of Meikle Mulltaggart.

With no path, the descent into the next col (Nick of the Saddle) will need another compass bearing in mist. A fence leads up Cairnsmore to a stile, after which head straight uphill to the flat gravelly summit. It is marked by a large cairn, a trig pillar, the remains of a small stone hut and a memorial to crashed aeroplanes.

The route now returns to Meikle Mulltaggart: on the first descent to Nick of the Saddle, keep a little east of the true direction (northeast) to meet the guiding fence that comes in from the right. Meikle Mulltaggart can be skirted on the left, or recrossed.

Cross the grassy saddle to 587m Millfore (unnamed). 400yds northeast is a cairn, and this marks the stile in the hidden fence just over the brow beyond. A small path leads east down the gentle ridge.

After a mile ($1^{1}/_{2}$km) the ridge steepens and becomes rocky, especially on its right-hand flank. So avoid difficulties on the left where necessary. Join the stream to cross the broken wall into the

WALK 6: 3 Cairnsmore from Talnotry

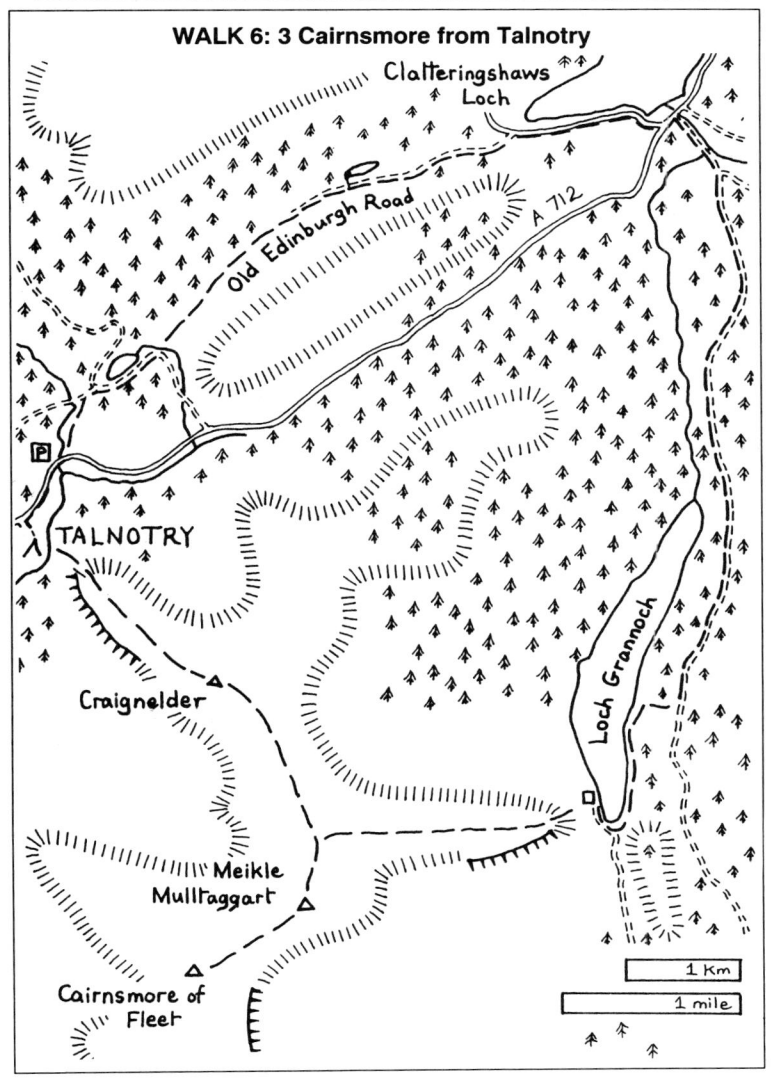

THE LOWTHER HILLS

pinewood around Loch Grannoch Lodge, and go down past a small waterfall to the Lodge itself, now an outdoor centre.

Turn right onto the track, and follow it to emerge from the mature pines at the head of the loch. Walk along the beach, and then take to the boggy eastern shore. After a slow mile, a ride leads up on the right to a forest road (unsurfaced). Follow this to the left, for $3^{1}/_{2}$ miles ($5^{1}/_{2}$km), to the A712 below the high intimidating dam of Clatteringshaws reservoir.

Turn left down the road for 300yds, and take the minor road on the right that rises to run alongside the loch. At the head of the first deep bay, a wide, smooth forest road branches off left. Follow this for $1^{1}/_{2}$ miles ($2^{1}/_{2}$km), until a wide and fairly muddy path leads ahead through a low pass in the hills. This descends first to left of the Black Strand stream, then to right, and enters young trees at the bottom of the valley.

After $^{1}/_{4}$ mile (400m) the path, now clearly a former track, emerges into a clearing, and now a small path goes down left to a crossing of the Tonderghie Burn (optimistically labelled 'Stepping Stones' on OL map). Go between low branches to the forest road beyond, and turn right to pass along the southern shore of Black Loch.

After another 400yds, the forest road crosses the Grey Mare's Tail Burn at a concrete bridge. It's worth making a short diversion upstream to visit the upper falls, then go downstream on a path to left of the stream. This bends right to a viewpoint above a waterfall pool. Soon afterwards, a small, steep path down right descends directly to the largest of the waterfalls, while the main path goes down more gently to the roadside.

Walk 6:4
TALNOTRY TRAIL
3 miles 750ft (5km 250m)
Waymarked paths: easy

Two waterfalls, a clifftop view, absolutely no tussocks or heather, and two summits if you want them - and all in only 3 miles (5km). The forest trail at Talnotry offers everything you want except, perhaps, distance.

One or two of Galloway's 700 wild goats can sometimes be seen on

CAIRNSMORE OF FLEET

this walk. If not, there are usually several hanging around next to the road in the goat park just east of the car park.

MAP: OL 32 (Galloway) or Landranger 77 (Dalmellington)

START/FINISH: Grey Mare's Tail car park, immediately east of Talnotry Campsite (GR 491721)

❋ ❋ ❋

Cross the road bridge and head up along the east side of the stream to the lowest and finest of the waterfalls. You can now take a steep and scrambly path uphill to the higher, waymarked path, or else return to the roadside for the official start of that same path.

The waymarks are blue-topped posts. The path heads upstream, and crosses a forest road, before climbing steeply in zigzags beside more waterfalls. Above the falls, the path follows the stream for another 400yds, then crosses it at a footbridge and climbs between trees. Here the ground has been scraped of bog to reveal bare bedrock, an enjoyable walking surface.

The path levels, and a boggy ride on the right can be used to gain the open hill and the small but heathery summit of Fell of Talnotry. This excursion is optional. The path continues across the slope, then descends to a forest road. Here turn right for $^1/_4$ mile ($^1/_2$km), before turning left again onto a path over tree-roots. All is clearly waymarked, and built up with rough gravel over boggy bits.

The path drops steeply beside a stream, then climbs on wooden steps to traverse above small crags. Here is a viewpoint indicator; the indicated view is between and over the trees to the rocky slopes of Craignelder.

After a gradual descent, the path meets a narrow cross-track. Turn right, downhill, to reach the roadside opposite the campsite.

Back at the car park, the short but steep ascent to Murray's Monument gives another view, and brings the day's total ascent up to the thousand-foot count. Murray himself was a self-taught son of a shepherd who became Professor of Oriental Languages at Edinburgh at the age of 36 but died a year later in 1813.

Walk 6:5
CAIRNSMORE OF DEE, FELL OF FLEET
13¹/₂ miles (3¹/₂ final forest road) 3100ft (22km 950m)
Rough hill-tops, forest rides, track: hard

A green tide of trees washes over the eastern part of this range, with only the most assertive hills managing to raise their heads above the needles. Cairnsmore of Dee is a rocky knob, and for those who like a challenge, the crossing of the three Cairnsmores by way of the Rhinns of Kells is an energetic high tramp for a long summer's day. Fell of Fleet, though lower, is just as wild, with its loch hidden among granite outcrops and yellow bog-grasses.

All between is trees. All in all, then, this is an austere walk, of the sort that could be called a "bash". I have found it most suitable for scouring away the whisky fumes and other old-year residues on the first of January. A bit of sleet suits the mood of this particular route.

The crossing of the Black Water of Dee can be impossible after heavy rain, which gives an excuse for shortening the walk by an escape along the Raiders' Road. Alternatively, it can be combined with Walk 6:3 for an outing of 24 miles, 5500ft, and two Cairnsmores (38km, 1700m, still only two Cairnsmores).

MAP: Landranger 77 (Dalmellington) or OL 32 (Galloway)
START/FINISH: Car park at Clatteringshaws Deer Museum (GR 552763)

❋ ❋ ❋

Cross the A712 road, to take the forest road uphill and left. Where a ruined dyke alongside the road turns uphill, follow it to rejoin the higher road. Where this road leaves the trees, head straight uphill to the high tower on Benniguinea.

Rough grassland runs down northwest into the broad col. The slope is dotted with self-seeded spruce, escapees from the plantation below, and this semi-wild tree cover is quite attractive. Look back

CAIRNSMORE OF FLEET

from the col to the fierce outline of the Benniguinea crags, an effect soon lost as height is gained on the way up to Cairnsmore of Dee. This climb is rough and rocky.

The Rig of Craig Gilbert is a wild one, with much bare rock. It

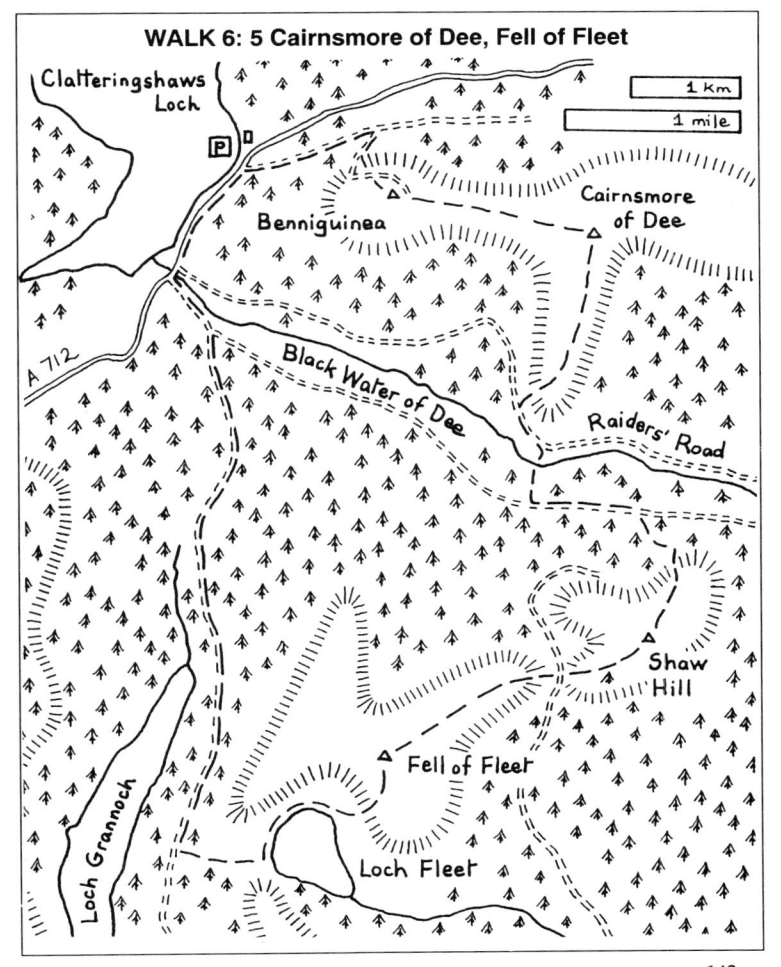

WALK 6: 5 Cairnsmore of Dee, Fell of Fleet

THE LOWTHER HILLS

leads down southward into the heart of the tree-wilderness. At the end of the open ground, head down southwest, between clear-felled and mature plantation, to the forest road. This is the Raiders' Road, where modern motorists can retrace the route of ancient drovers and cattle-thieves, and a right turn along it is a straightforward exit from the walk.

Turn left along the Raiders' Road for 400yds, until a clearing on the right allows access to the riverbank. Here it is usually possible to ford the Black Water at the island (GR 579735). A stick from the forest is a useful aid.

The forest road parallel with the river is reached through open forest. Turn left (east) for ¾ mile (1km), then turn uphill on an unplanted ride, which is very rough. This runs up to a stone wall in the middle of the tree belt. Follow the wall, left and slightly rising, to its highest point at GR 593728, where a stream runs under it. Go straight uphill along a narrow ride to emerge onto the open slopes of Shaw Hill.

From Shaw Hill's top follow open ground towards the Nick of Orchars, and take the left-hand of two rides. A forest road runs through the Nick. The correct ride will bring you onto this road at the saddle-point: but if you reach the road elsewhere, simply turn uphill to that saddle. Now a wide ride runs west to a large clearing with a tall square cairn in. The top of the clearing opens onto the Fell of Fleet, for a rough climb to its summit.

Go straight down the back of the hill to the shore of Loch Fleet. A small path runs to the right around the loch, passing various pieces of measuring apparatus. This is one of the lochs most affected by acidification, though it is not yet clear whether this is entirely due to acid rain or whether spruce needles also play a part.

The path leads over a low shoulder (GR 556698) and down through the trees beside a ruined wall. At the forest road below, turn right for 3½ miles (5½km) to the A712 below the Clatteringshaws dam. The reservoir shore beside the road leads back to the Deer Museum.

CAIRNSMORE OF FLEET

Walk 6:6
WHITHORN COAST and ST NINIAN'S CAVE
11 miles 18km
Path, clifftop and road: easy/moderate

The Whithorn peninsula is the home of St Ninian, who landed here from Ireland in AD398 to set up the first organised Christian community in Northern Europe. The clifftop walk links the cave where he went to reflect and pray with the chapel at Isle of Whithorn, the pilgrim port. The third sacred site, his priory at Whithorn itself, can be visited on the drive in to the start of the walk.

Some of the clifftop path is narrow, and close to the crumbling cliff edge.

MAP: Landranger 83 (Newton Stewart)

START/FINISH: at a small car park near Physgill House: signposts from Whithorn say "St Ninian's Cave" (GR 432366)

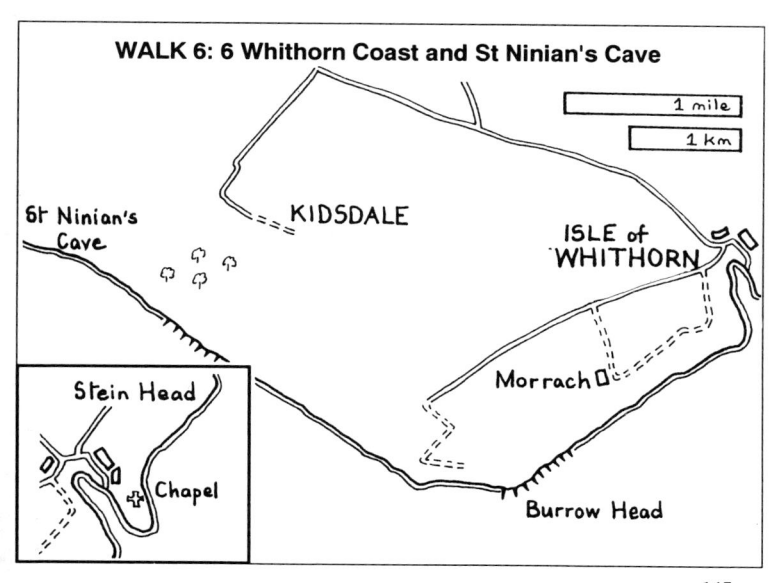

❋ ❋ ❋

THE LOWTHER HILLS

From the car park continue along the track, past the farm, to a sign pointing right "St Ninian's Cave". A wide path leads down alongside a stream, through a sunken wood of sycamores. After a mile (1½km), the path emerges suddenly into the light as it reaches the foreshore.

The cave is visible on the right, and is reached by walking along the pebbly beach. Various carved stones that used to stand in the cave are now at the Discovery Centre in Whithorn. Those stones date from the eighth century - by which time Ninian himself had already been gone for 400 years.

Return along the foreshore, continuing past the arrival-path for 50yds, across the mouth of a second tiny valley, then scrambling up onto the grassy clifftop. A fence is just below. Follow the clifftop for 2 miles (3km). Walls running across have stone step-stiles. Though the cliffs are not high, the way that the bedding plane of the rock has been tilted to the vertical means that the shore is eroded into combs and finger-shapes, with small stacks and deep inlets. England, Ireland and Man are visible across the water, and the small rock of Scares.

You pass above a nasty rubbish tip, and here a gate leads into the caravan site. Walk round the seaward side of this to a wide grey gate, then back right, alongside a broken wall, to regain the clifftop.

At the end of the wall, a railing-stile leads onto the cliff edge. A small path runs outside the barbed wire, along the very brink. As the wire is two strands only, it is not impossible to roll through to the inside of the fence. The way passes above inlets with interesting rock-scenery, although the Devil's Bridge is not visible from above. The white tower at Isle of Whithorn comes into sight ahead, and the cliffs become lower, then give way to earth bank, and here the way ahead is blocked by brambles. A wheelmark track runs left, towards Morrach farm, and reaches its access track by way of a cattle grid.

Turn right along the farm track, and at its end, down right into Isle of Whithorn. Here are hotels, inns and a shop, as well as the site of Ninian's chapel. A cairn (the Witness Cairn) invites you to add a stone: those treating the expedition as a pilgrimage will bring their stone, perhaps a particularly heavy one, from the start of the walk.

If time, and the attractions of the pubs and cafes, permits, a short further excursion can be made to Stein Head. This path starts at the furthest corner of an estate of sheltered housing. A stile over a low stone wall marks its beginning.

Leave Isle of Whithorn by the same road, but instead of turning into the farm track, keep ahead, following signs to the caravan site, for a quicker return. Pass through the site, to reverse the first part of the walk back to the car park.

7: Outlying Hills

Isolated hills can't help having wide views. They also tend to have their own geology, and so their own characters that are different from the hill groups they lie apart from.

Cairn Table is a little chip of North Yorkshire, transported into the South Ayrshire industrial landscape: or rather, not a chip but a dollop. Peat and sandstone make a sombre hill.

Tinto is unique: arguably not a Southern Upland hill at all as it lies across the boundary fault and so is actually the second highest point of the Central Lowlands. (Ben Cleuch, in the Ochils, is 14m higher.) Tinto is a tall pile of pink gravel.

The hills of Roxburghshire, lying between Hawick and Langholm, rise to 2000ft at a single point. The steep grassy sides of Cauldcleuch Head are fine, but its flat, soggy, peaty top is not. To the south lies a range of similar hills that are little, and little climbed. Again, their fine sides belie their rough peaty tops. I offer a couple more walks, one based on the handsome town of Langholm, and leave the remainder for those who like to plunge, knee-deep in heather, into the unknown.

Walk 7:1
* CAIRN TABLE and the OLD SANQUHAR ROAD
9 miles 1800ft (14km 500m)
Wet path, heather hillside, bog and track: moderate/hard

---

*I like this walk: I like its uncompromising nature. However, many may not share my taste for heather bog and stones; so a warning is attached to the star * I have given the route for quality. Cairn Table is a dark hill of peat and heather, set in a sombre industrial landscape of coal and iron. It is distinguished by its rocky top, and by the tall cairn set there.*

Cairn Table is a popular ascent among the inhabitants of South Ayrshire, and the path up to it is reasonably clear and easy, although wet. Behind Cairn Table the country is empty and heathery, with some striking peat-hags. A short rough crossing leads to the old drove road between Muirkirk and Sanquhar, and this gives a straightforward return

OUTLYING HILLS

journey.

MAP: Landranger 71 (Lanark)

From the traffic lights at the centre of Muirkirk, a minor road leads across the valley and through opencast workings to Kames. There is car

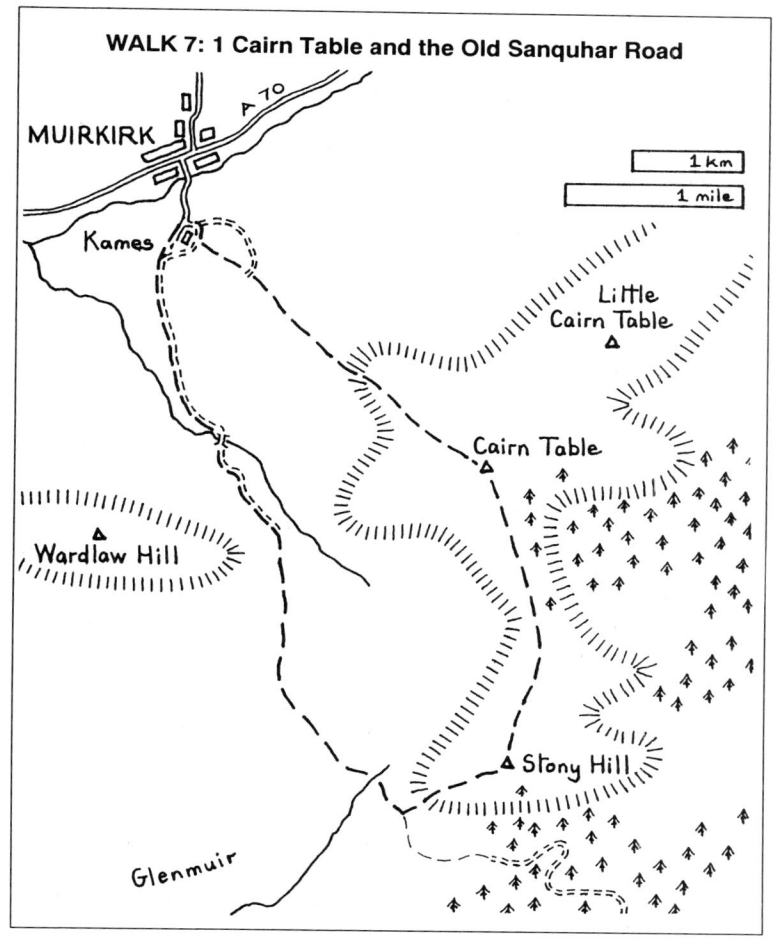

WALK 7: 1 Cairn Table and the Old Sanquhar Road

THE LOWTHER HILLS

parking space at the tall red building that is the former railway station.
START/FINISH: Kames (GR 697264)

※ ※ ※

Attached to the station is a row of cottages, "Ironworks Cotts". Just before them, a rough track heads uphill then bends right. After 200yds is a concrete hut containing dangerous chemicals, and behind it is a small gate onto the hill.

Head uphill, on a faint path, passing to left of a white ruin, and then to left of a length of brick wall. Now the path is clearer, and marked with white concrete posts, as it winds uphill among the hummocks of former workings. It crosses the top end of a track, and heads uphill with a ruined wall and fence on its left.

The slope is gentle, but the going is peaty and often wet. Still with the fence on its left, the path climbs the steeper slope of the Steel, becoming stony as it does so. Small outcrops of grey sandstone begin to appear on the approach to the final cairn.

The summit has rock outcrops, a trig point and an ancient cairn. But its most notable feature is the high triangular memorial cairn. It was clearly visible from the valley below, and turns out to be a good 5m (15ft or more) in height. It commemorates the dead of the First World War. The peaty surroundings and the sandstone outcrop recall certain hills of the northern Pennines, such as Nine Standards. But the surrounding moor will be found less harsh.

One hundred yards southwest of the summit is the famous summit spring. White-painted rocks and a small path lead to it. It is equipped with a tin mug on a chain. (A path continues downhill from the spring; it can be followed almost to the Capel Water. This is a short way onto the track used for the final part of the walk.)

From the ancient cairn head south. A small cairned path leads down slopes of short heather, interrupted by an area of bare stones and gravel. Forestry plantations rise from the left to the ridgeline, and the path follows the boundary fence down into the wet col below.

Here the path is lost. Trees are still alongside on the left as you leave the col. This first climb is tough and heathery, but then come patches of grass, as well as quad bike wheelmarks beside the fence. This fence leads onto the summit plateau of Stony Hill. Here is an impressive peat-hag: piles of black topped by orange grass, with spreading silver pools between. This can be appreciated in comfort from behind the fence, which takes a line avoiding hags. At a fence T-junction, turn left for 100yds onto the grass of the northeast top, which carries an anemometer mast. The shallow col leading to the main, southwest, top has peat-hags, but these can be walked round on the left.

From the small cairn, head southwest on grass, aiming towards the remote valley head of Glenmuir. The ground steepens on the flank of Pepper Hill. A stone wall crosses below, and the path of the old drove road will be found running immediately above this. If you approach the path at any other point, you may well walk across it without seeing it.

Willie Cunningham, an eighteenth-century "pedestrian" (or long-distance walker), laid a bet that he could beat the stagecoach between Glasgow's Tron Steeple and Sanquhar. This path was the means of winning his wager. More recently, it was used by the long-distance runner Hugh Symonds on his way from Ben Lomond to Skiddaw during a record-breaking run over all the three-thousanders of Britain. The complete crossing from Sanquhar to Muirkirk is still occasionally walked, with a bus for the return. However, south of where we stand, the old path is forest track and tarred road, and is not recommended. Turning north, though, we now use its best stretch for the return to Muirkirk.

The path at first is faint, used mostly by the occasional shepherd on his quad bike. It dips in and out of the re-entrant of a stream and then climbs very gently across the moor, northwest. At the wide col between Wardlaw Hill and Stony Hill it starts to become clearer.

The path turns north as it descends, and after a mile (1$^{1/2}$km) becomes a stony track. A stout metal footbridge, the Sanquhar Brig, crosses the Capel Water. On the final approach to Kames, a tall triangular cairn comes into sight: smaller only than the one on Cairn Table. It commemorates the tar kiln of John Macadam, which stood here from 1786. It has a small bench for a final rest, although with the start point just $^{1}/_{2}$ mile ($^{3}/_{4}$km) away, this may not be required.

Walk 7:2
* TINTO HILL
4 miles 1600ft (6km 500m)
Path: easy

Fifteen hundred feet from car park to summit, and back down the same way: this one is hard work. There are compensations. Tinto rises 1500ft (500m) out of the green Clydesdale, with the River Clyde winding around its ankles like an affectionate pet snake. In such splendid isolation, it gives the walker a fine feeling of rising ever higher and higher above the countryside. On a clear day, the summit views are very wide indeed, even if they do not extend quite to Lochnagar and Knocklayd (Ireland). By the same token, Tinto can be seen, and identified, from much of the southern half of Scotland. This is useful when you want to point into the distance and say "I've climbed that."

The path does what it can to make the relentless ascent comfortable for you, and there is an enjoyable passage round the head of Maurice's Cleuch.

MAP: Landranger 72 (Upper Clyde)

Turn off the A73 near Thankerton at the Tinto Hill Tea Room. (The minor road opposite is signed to Thankerton.) After ¼ mile (½km) there is a car park on the left.

START/FINISH: Tinto Hill car park (GR 964374)

❊ ❊ ❊

Two grey gates lead out of the car park. Beside the right-hand one is a handsome kissing-gate bearing carved lettering "Tinto Hill". It leads onto a wide gravel path. The path leads over the heather moor between fences - it is quite literally over the moor, as it has been built up above the moor's dampness.

At a third kissing-gate it emerges onto open ground at the foot of Totherin Hill. Here, on the left, is an ancient fort, almost invisible from the path. If you walk up under the power line you'll find two deep concentric ditches.

The path heads up the right-hand flank of Totherin Hill, but here, to introduce variety, it's better to strike left and go straight up the face of the hill on patches of grass among the heather. As height is gained, the fort behind becomes very noticeable. From Totherin's

OUTLYING HILLS

cairn, a path rejoins the main path up Tinto: these few steps of downhill make a break from the unvarying up of that path.

The next bit of up is particularly unvarying, as the path, a wide pink scree, goes straight up the face of the hill. Just before the top of this steep section, the path divides. The lesser path on the right may be missed, but it is the one that includes the traverse round the head

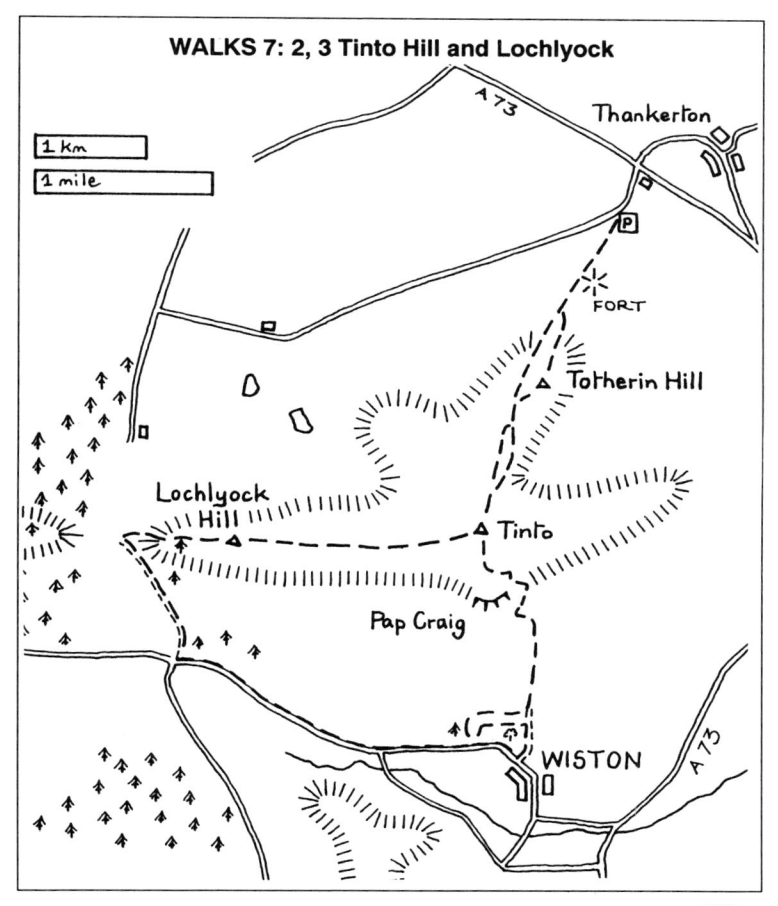

Tinto from Quothquan Law

of Maurice's Cleuch. Here the wide path crosses the top of a long steep slope of heather and pink scree.

A fence joins from the right, and escorts you up the final climb. Tinto's summit cairn is one of the largest in Scotland. Most of the work on it was done in the Bronze Age. We may imagine that early man found it necessary to send lookouts to the top to see if anyone was coming to attack the fort he'd made at the bottom. The top of Tinto is often in the cloud, and one day the lookouts, to pass the time, idly started to pile stones...

The very top of Tinto is a viewpoint table that claims to see Knocklayd Hill in the mountains of Antrim, 106 miles (170km) away. One point that is visible is Ben Cleuch in the Ochils, 41 miles (66km) away. An odd distortion in the space-time of southern Scotland could be deduced from the fact that, on Ben Cleuch's viewpoint table, the distance to Tinto Hill is $41^{1}/_{2}$ miles.

Return down the same path, with fence on left, for 300yds. If you missed Maurice's Cleuch on the way up, you'll want to make sure of getting it on the way down. So at this point, take the left-hand path, which stays close beside the fence while the main path, which

OUTLYING HILLS

is much wider and stonier, bears away slightly right.

After the wide steep scree-path, ignore branch-paths on the right: the first is marked "No Public Right-of-Way", the next two are to the cairn on Totherin Hill. Stay on the main path back to the car park.

Walk 7:3
TINTO by PAP CRAIG, with LOCHLYOCK
7$^{1/2}$ miles 1700ft (12km 500m)
Steep path and grassy hill, 2 miles road to finish: moderate
See map p153

Distance and climb here are similar to Walk 7:2, but there's an important difference. That walk went up and down by a moderately steep path. This goes up by the steepest possible route, and down by the gentlest.

Pap Craig is a rocky place perched high on the side of the hill - there is even a possibility of a little scrambling on its face. The top part of the hill is bare pink gravel. This is a more challenging and more interesting way than Walk 7:1, and its only drawback is the 2 miles of road at the end. Perhaps there is an athlete in the party who can be persuaded to jog ahead for the car while the rest of you recline and watch the paragliders on Lochlyock Hill.

MAP: Landranger 72 (Upper Clyde)

Parking in Wiston village, or on the verge of the B7055 at the village edge.

START/FINISH: Wiston Lodge YMCA (GR 956322)

❋ ❋ ❋

Walk up the driveway of Wiston Lodge, and pass left of the buildings onto the uphill track, which is signed "Tinto Hill". After the open camping field on the left the track enters mixed woods. Just after some stone farm buildings, a green track runs off to the left. This is the start of the Nature Trail through the woods.

The Nature Trail takes $^{1/2}$ mile ($^{3/4}$km) to get you 100yds further up the track. But with Tinto looking intimidating, you may appreciate $^{1/2}$ mile of flattish going. After 300yds, turn off the green track to

THE LOWTHER HILLS

cross a log footbridge on the left. The path wanders down through the trees, crosses a small stream and wanders back up through the trees. It passes a clearing with a rough wooden cross for outdoor worship, and an artificial pond. It rejoins the top of the main track.

Here a metal gate, with stile alongside, leads out of the trees into the corner of a field. Go up, with wall on the right, to another gate and stile. This second field is very muddy, which is a shame, as the actual hill path ahead is grassy and dry. Still with wall on the right, go up through two more gates. The wall on the right becomes a fence, and the path crosses it by a wide bench-stile onto the open hill.

The path is grassy and not heavily used. It slants up right, below the scree and rock of the Pap Craig: a direct assault on the Pap offers steep heather and scree and some scrappy scrambling. The path, once out from under the crag, zigzags up steep grass, to gain the flat ground at the crag's top. (The summit viewpoint of Tinto will mention Lochnagar, 95 miles away. And Lochnagar too has its little bump on the side, the Meikle Pap. However, I can devise no other points of correspondence between pink Tinto and dark Lochnagar.)

From the top of the Pap, strike right, up bare gravel, to join a fence - actually two fences side by side with a trace of path between. A stile at the top leads out to the summit cairn.

From the summit head westwards, which is towards "Goatfell, 60 miles". Pass the trig point and go down grassy slopes with a wall on the left. The grass and wall lead gently down and along to the unmarked summit of Lochlyock Hill. When the wind is right, paraglidists leap off Lochlyock Hill.

The wall leads on westwards, soon with a new plantation on the left. At the plantation's end is a stile on the left. A short steep slope leads down to a gravel track. Follow this down to the road below.

Turn left, along the road signposted "Wiston $2^{1/4}$", and fork left after a mile ($1^{1/2}$km) at another sign for Wiston.

OUTLYING HILLS

Walk 7:4
CAULDCLEUCH HEAD
7 miles 1600ft (11km 500m)
Grassy ridges and swampy summit: moderate

It is sometimes said that the least interesting point on any hill is its summit. This perverse assertion is certainly true of Cauldcleuch Head. Its top is a wide flat bog, where three galvanised fences meet at an ugly gate. Its only distinction is in being just over 2000 feet high - the spot-height at 608m/1996ft is not the top, but lies 1/4 mile (1/2km) east of it.

The sides of the hill are better. The approach is along the deep, green Hermitage Valley. The grim keep of Hermitage Castle reminds that this ground was once inhabited by a sept of cattle-thieves as accomplished as any in Scotland. Steep slopes and a well-defined grassy ridge lead up into the summit swamp. A deep little stream hollow leads back out again.

MAP: Landranger 79 (Hawick and Eskdale)

EXTENSION: This can be combined with Walk 7:5, giving eleven tops in the day - but you'll have to work for them.

START/FINISH: 3 miles (5km) west of Hermitage Castle, the road climbs to a high point on Bught Shank. Here a small quarry offers parking space (GR 459972)

※ ※ ※

Walk east along the road to a small plantation above. A track turns uphill along its front edge but this is ignored (this track, running up the Gorrenberry Burn, is the alternative route if sensitive livestock might be disturbed on the start of the main route). Continue past the plantation to take a track up beside its further, eastern, edge.

The track immediately turns down right, and becomes undefined as it descends a field to two wooden gates and a ford of the Gorrenberry Burn. Now it climbs in clear zigzags up the face of Dod Hill. As the slope eases the track becomes a green path that leads to a fence corner at the top of the hill.

This fence is followed, left, along the green ridge of Crossbow Hill and up rougher ground onto Muckle Land Knowe. The fence bends right on the plateau, with the actual summit of Muckle Land

THE LOWTHER HILLS

somewhere in the surrounding bog. The fence leads on to the summit of Cauldcleuch Head.

Continue northwards along the same fence. The ground soon becomes drier. As it flattens again, the fence bends left, then divides. Take the left branch, southwest, along the well-defined ridge towards Langtae Hill.

At the low point of the ridge, before the slight rise to Langtae, turn down left on a steepish grassy slope to the Langtae Sike burn. Follow this downstream, crossing frequently: the moving water has exposed grey rock, showing that the hill is not, in fact, merely a big heap of peat.

After $^1/_4$ mile ($^1/_2$km) is a stream junction, and the start of a rough track. This gradually becomes wider and stonier. Where it fords the

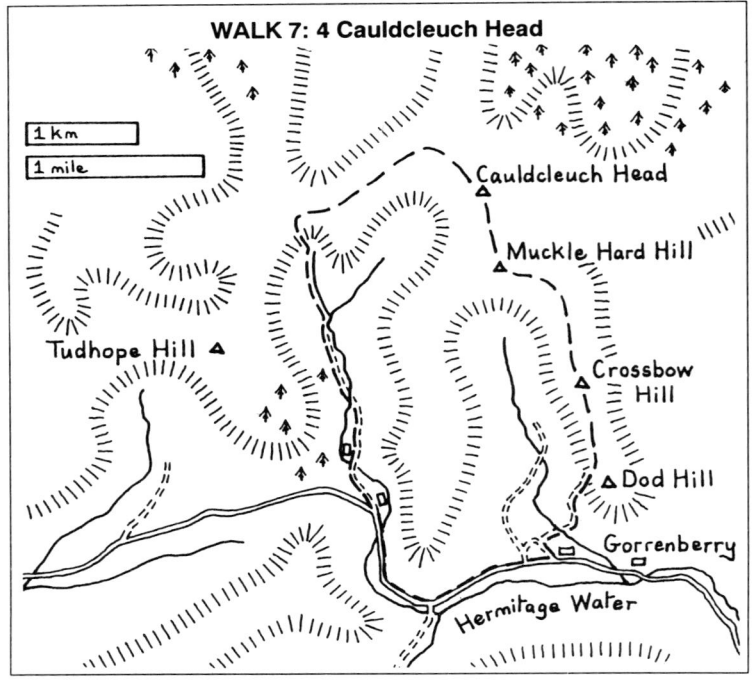

OUTLYING HILLS

stream, remain on the left bank, as the track soon recrosses at a second ford. The track soon emerges from its little glen to join the road at Billhope. Turn left for a mile (1½km) to the start-point.

Walk 7:5
CIRCUIT of TWISLEHOPE HOPE
9 miles 1200ft (14km 350m)

The hills above the Ewes Water look grand on the map: contour lines are brown and crowded, and there is a multitude of little summits with names like Cockplay and Carlintooth. They look grand from the trunk road A7.

They are not quite as grand as they look. The summits are boggy, or else heathery, and rather flat. The going is heavy. The main pleasure is in the folded shapes of the surrounding stream valleys. This is a good walk in bad weather, as the pointed-looking (but actually flat) peaks alternately loom close and then become big and distant behind sheets of rain. In mist, though, it is a grim little expedition.

Grim, but - the name suggests - not altogether hopeless. A "Hope" is in fact a summer pasture in a sheltered high valley.

MAP: Landranger 79 (Hawick)

EXTENSION: This one can be combined with Walk 7:4 (Cauldcleuch) for a really tiring day in the hills.

At the top of the Hermitage Valley road, 400yds west of the plantation edge, there is parking space in a roadside quarry. There is also verge parking at the Twislehope track end.

START/FINISH: Carewood Rig (GR 434976)

❊ ❊ ❊

Walk east along the road to the plantation, and turn back uphill alongside a fence - this is the line of the regional boundary. A gate leads through to the summit of Geordie's Hill, where a few stones have been gathered into a vestigial cairn.

Go back through the fence, and head downhill westwards: surprisingly there is no guiding fence now, even though we are marching the boundary where Dumfries & Galloway meets the Borders Region. The wide col below is Guile Hass - here is Nordic

THE LOWTHER HILLS

nomenclature, "Hass" being the familiar Lakeland word "Hause", meaning a pass. A rough slope leads to the heathery Tamond Heights.

Easier grass leads through the col of Stockcleuch Edge, then it's more heather over Mid Hill. Quad bike wheelmarks assist through the following col, and the ridge called Unthank Pikes is short heather and enjoyable walking. A fallen dyke leads to the summit of Pike Hill.

Two electric fences lead down left: turn down to left of the left-hand one, southeast. The fence guides through the col and up onto Scaw'd Bank, and continues along the flat ridge of the Pikes. (The Norsemen here had a very different idea of what constitutes a "Pike" from their cousins in Cumbria!)

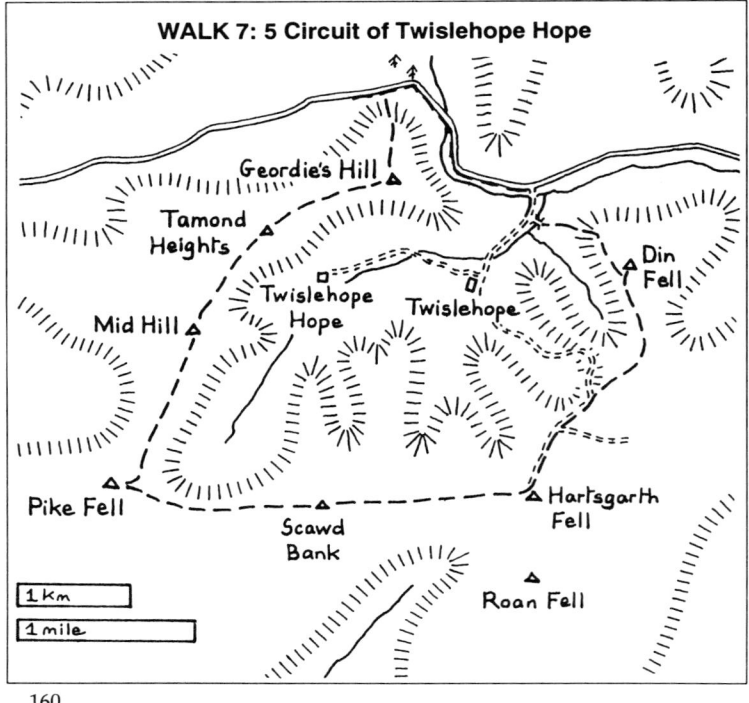

WALK 7: 5 Circuit of Twislehope Hope

OUTLYING HILLS

The fence branches at the ill-defined high point of Hartsgarth Fell. The heathery, boggy, flat top of Roan Fell is $^{1}/_{2}$ mile ($^{3}/_{4}$km) south down the fence. I cannot recommend the diversion to that unappealing spot. Instead, turn down left from the fence junction, to the top end of a stony track. Follow this northeast for a mile (1$^{1}/_{4}$km), until it bends left (west) above the head of the Caulker Grain.

The main descent route here leaves the track to contour northeast, crossing rough wet heather to join a ridgeline fence north of Haregrain Rig. The fence leads up the slope of Din Fell, to a gate 300yds southeast of its summit. Go through the gate to climb the gentle slope to the trig point. This has heather-free grass to lounge about on while enjoying the view eastwards to the Cheviots, with the square black keep of Hermitage Castle directly below.

Return through the fence gate, to go down a grassy slope beside the fence. When the road appears below (9 contour lines up from the bottom of the slope) turn left, away from the fence, towards the Twislehope Burn. There is a footbridge hidden in hazel and alder, 300yds from where the track crosses the main valley stream to the road.

(A more adventurous way down from the track on Haregrain Rig to the Twislehope Burn, is to descend the stream between Ewe Hill and Din Fell. A sheep path runs above the stream on the right, but then you must drop to the stream bed to pass through a mildly rocky section.)

Turn left up the road for 1$^{1}/_{2}$ miles (2$^{1}/_{2}$km) to the walk's startpoint.

Walk 7:6
* WHITA HILL at LANGHOLM
6$^{1}/_{2}$ miles 1200ft (10$^{1}/_{2}$km 350m)
Path, road, rough heather hill: moderate

Three rivers meet at the grey town of Langholm. The three river valleys, with various low passes through the hills between them, will have confused English cattle owners seeking to recover their stolen property without the benefit of the Landranger map. The town is an attractive

THE LOWTHER HILLS

MacDiarmaid memorial sculpture on Whita Hill

centre for short walks along the river-banks. The surrounding hills are shapely, but too low for serious hill-walking. One escapes with relief from the heathery tops, only to get entangled in cow pastures on the grassy sides.

The walk I give here could be considered a mere urban constitutional. But the burghers of Langholm are descended from sturdy reivers (cattle-thieves), and their Sunday stroll is liable to be an energetic one.

Meanwhile, true hill enthusiasts, spurred on by my assertion of poor hill-walking, will construct themselves an even more energetic outing over ten or a dozen of the pointy little tops. They might be tempted by the six trig points in the hills immediately around the town...

MAP: Landranger 79 (Hawick)

START/FINISH: New Langholm, with street parking at the western end of the footbridge over the Esk River (GR 362845)

※　※　※

Parking on the wrong side of the river allows the walk to start across the wide footbridge. It was "Young Lochinvar" in Walter Scott's

OUTLYING HILLS

poem who swam the Esk River, where ford there was none. He was not alone in doing so, as the river was an important strategic feature in the cross-border raiding ground. In later years, young couples flying to Gretna had to decide whether to wait for the tides of Solway or go for the ford at Longtown: a tricky tactical decision with angry parents in hot pursuit.

Bear right into Charles Street Old to the town's main square, and head out on the A7 (Carlisle) road. At the end of the town this bends right, and a tarred lane, Hall Path, runs ahead. After passing houses, it becomes a rough track at a gate.

The track runs up through a wood of oak and birch, with the Esk River seen through the trees. Ignore a path signed "Jenny Noble's Gill" descending right. After a mile (1½km) the track emerges from

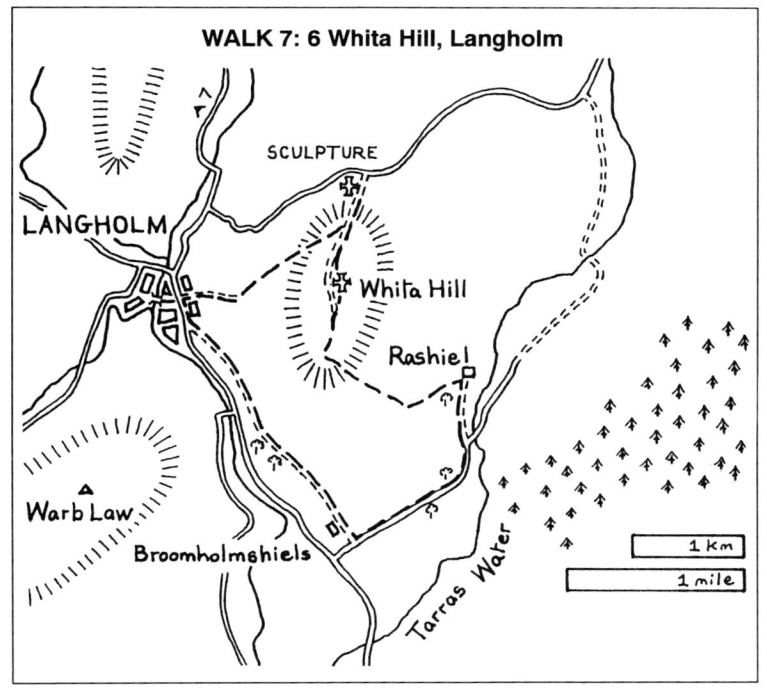

WALK 7: 6 Whita Hill, Langholm

THE LOWTHER HILLS

the trees. On the map a path slants up left here, following the line of the low-voltage power lines, but it cannot be seen on the ground. So stay on the Hall Path track through Broomholmshiels to the hill road beyond.

The road leads up over the shoulder of Whita Hill into the lonely Tarras glen. This secluded valley is good for hiding cows in, and the trees beside the stream remedy the bleakness of the upper slopes. After a mile (1½km) the road bends right over a bridge which it crosses "at its own risk", but here the track for Rashiel farm runs forward. Pass to right of the first two farm buildings, then bend back left. The hill path starts off past the farm's brick water tank, then becomes faint as it slants uphill slightly south of east. It passes above the top end of a stream-side wood, to join a ruined wall running directly uphill.

Comparatively easy going is found alongside the wall. At the ridge of Whita Hill the broken wall bends right to a railed gateway in an intact wall. Cross the railings in the gateway, to a path leading to the wireless masts. A track leads on to the tall monument on the hill's summit.

This tall structure commemorates Major General John Maxwell (Knight of the Garter, Knight of the Persian Order of the Lion and the Sun, Fellow of the Royal Society, etc. etc.). After reading his exemplary life, as carved into the column, your only wonder will be that they didn't build his monument even bigger.

Whita is the southernmost of the hills, and views southwards are across the plains to England. The country there is obviously fertile and full of fat cattle, just waiting to be driven north across the border. To the helpful complications of any border country was added the special convenience of a territory, the "Debatable Lands", under the control of neither government. Twelve miles (20km) of lower Liddesdale was ruled only by the reiving Armstrong family.

Starting beside the summit wall, a small path leads northwards and is preferable to the stony track alongside. The ground is a hummocky mixture of grass and heather. The path joins the track for the final descent to the road pass. Here is another monument: a sculpture of iron and bronze commemorating Hugh MacDiarmid the poet. One of his verses is inscribed on the cairn nearby.

MacDiarmid wrote so much that the best stuff tends to get

OUTLYING HILLS

submerged. The short poem *Scotland Small?* is a good entry to his work, and hillwalkers should also enjoy the mountain portrait *Liathach*.

Return up the track for 500yds, and look for a branch path on the right. (This path is clearer on the left, where it arrives through a gate in the fence alongside.) The path runs around the hill, gently descending alongside a grassy gully. It runs under pylons, and joins a path descending directly from the Maxwell monument into Langholm. Turn downhill, through a gate with stile onto a track that goes down through the golf course. It becomes a steep tarred path that arrives suddenly, as "Kirk Wynd", in Langholm's main square.

Walk 7:7
ANNAN BANKS to BURNSWARK
Expedition: Annan to Burnswark - 17 miles 1000ft (27km 300m)
Expedition, but bus back from Ecclefechan - $11^{1/2}$ miles 1000ft (18km 300m)
** Annan banks: to Brydekirk and back - 6 miles (10km)
* Burnswark from road end - $^{1}/_{2}$ mile 200ft ($^{1}/_{4}$km 60m)
All walks: paths and minor roads: easy

Burnswark is a small but interesting hill, with Roman remains on top, and extensive views all round. However, it's a hill drive rather than a hill walk. A road runs to within $^{1}/_{4}$ mile ($^{1}/_{2}$km) of the summit.

A half-mile hill walk really is too short. So I've gone to the opposite extreme. By starting from Annan, Burnswark becomes a major expedition, and one of the longest walks in the book. There is still that road, which now has to be walked up: but there are also two pubs, 4 miles (7km) of lovely riverbank, and a notable Birthplace at Ecclefechan. Those not interested in Carlyle's great historical work Sartor Resartus may still want to pay respects to him as a walker; as a young man he travelled on foot from here to Edinburgh to enrol at the University. (That trip, if taken by way of Langholm, the Culter Fells, the Manor Hills and the Pentlands, is a worthwhile one for today's walker, and starts over Burnswark.)

There are inns at Brydekirk (Brig Inn) and Ecclefechan (Ecclefechan Hotel). Carlyle's Birthplace is under the care of the National Trust for Scotland, and is open May-September on weekdays. Buses link Ecclefechan and Brydekirk with Annan, the last one back being mid-afternoon.

THE LOWTHER HILLS

MAP: Landranger 85 (Carlisle)

As you leave Annan, the last street on the right before the bridge is Battery Street. At its foot is a car park.

START/FINISH: Annan, car park just east of bridge GR 193666

✽ ✽ ✽

The riverside walk up the east (true left) bank starts as a tarred path past football pitches. To loosen up for the expedition ahead, you can attempt the contortions of the 'Trim Circuit' on various bits of apparatus beside the path. At the end of the park the riverside path becomes grassy or muddy, depending on the season. It passes under the bypass. After another ³/₄ mile (1km), at the end of a footbridge, it passes round to right of a transformer station then returns to the riverbank. Upstream, it passes through woodland where red squirrels may be seen. Anywhere along the river you will find herons: I saw five between Annan and Ecclefechan.

The path becomes track, then reaches road at the bridge into Brydekirk. Continue on the same (east) bank - the path becomes less marked, but stays by the river. Soon the not-terribly-towering summit of Burnswark appears ahead. At the junction with the Mein Water follow the sidestream's bank to a gate onto the minor road. Cross the old stone bridge and take a right fork to reach Ecclefechan.

Leave Ecclefechan by the street to right of the hotel. It ends at the motorway, which is crossed by a footbridge. (This is still marked as a road bridge on Landranger.) Turn left at the roundabout, and right to pass the Kirkconnel Hall Hotel. The narrow road leads uphill, with widening views behind. Turn left at a radio mast on the way up.

The road enters a plantation and becomes a track. At a track T-junction (GR 187784) is parking space for one or two cars. (This is the start-point for the short walk of Burnswark on its own.) Take neither side-track, but keep ahead on a path between the trees that climbs to a gate onto the open hill. A zig-zag to the right and back left is the gentlest way onto the summit of Burnswark.

Burnswark isn't a real Pictish fort, but a replica built by the Romans so they could practise attacking it.

Return by the same route to Ecclefechan and by the first section

OUTLYING HILLS

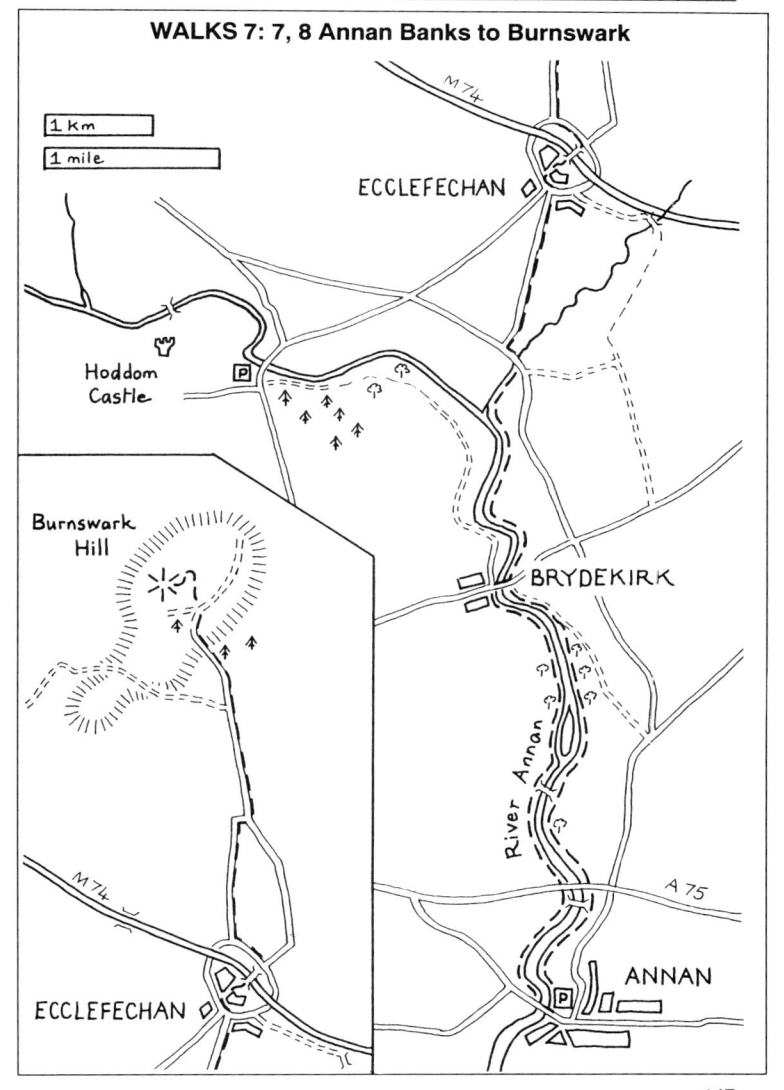

WALKS 7: 7, 8 Annan Banks to Burnswark

THE LOWTHER HILLS

of riverbank to Brydekirk. Cross the road bridge into the bottom of the village, and at once turn left into River Street to find the start of the riverside path.

After two miles it passes back under the by-pass and then joins a riverside track. Where this track turns up away from the river, watch out for the path, which is narrow between high willow-herb, continuing along the riverbank. It climbs stone steps onto the road at the end of the bridge leading into Annan.

Walk 7:8
* HODDOM CASTLE SHORT TRAILS
Up to 5 miles (8km)
Paths: easy
See map with route 7:7

START/FINISH: Car park near Hoddom Bridge, GR 163726

✻ ✻ ✻

At Hoddom is what is possibly the most salubrious caravan site in Scotland, with its own castle, golf-course and walking trails. The trails, through woodland and along the banks of the Annan, are very pleasingly laid out. A map can be obtained from the Warden's Office, which is also the shop. The map is necessary: the waymarking is rather patchy - the 'red route' in Woodcock Air isn't marked at all, and is only suitable for skilled navigators. There is another path, the Mainholm Farm Trail, that runs up the river's eastern bank to Brocklerigg Bridge.

The riverbanks of Walk 7:7 can also be used as a way from Annan to Hoddom.

* ANNAN BANKS TO HODDOM
12 miles (19km) for the return journey
riverside paths, and a pathless wood: easy/moderate

Start as on Walk 7:7 and follow the riverbank to Brydekirk. Cross the road bridge into Brydekirk, and take the first street on the right. It leads to the riverbank, and past Brydekirk Mains, to continue as concrete track past Upper Brydekirk. Where it turns left into Turnshawhead, keep ahead through a wooden gate and follow the left-hand edge of a field. A stile leads into Woodcock Air, which is a deciduous wood.

There is no particular path but the wood is open and walkable. Head west, to find a rutted track that runs above the river. When this reaches the B723, turn down right, to the lodge and entrance to Hoddom Castle grounds. Enter the grounds, and take a path on the right to the riverside. After 200yds beside the river, a path branching left is 'Ladies' Walk' and leads to the Castle.

APPENDIXES

A: LONGER OUTINGS

To walk for several days through this area can give a real sense of wild adventure. It's possible to pass most of a day without meeting a road, or a fellow-human. The country is real hill country, even if it is not as wild as the Highlands. Hotels and B&Bs are widely spaced, but there are several mountain bothies.

The Southern Upland Way

This is the least-walked of Britain's National Trails, with half a dozen parties a day at the height of the season. There is a good reason for this. Although the coast-to-coast line, with hills all the way, is inspiring, too much of the walk when you get down to it is on roads or under needle-trees. There is also a considerable accommodation problem on the long leg from St John's Town of Dalry to Sanquhar.

That said, the walk has some good points. It does offer the solitude you'd get by not being on a trail at all. It is well waymarked, and well maintained. It lets you cross the country quite quickly. And it does have splendid moments, even if these moments are rather too far apart.

There is much to be said for tackling the walk westbound. The easier ground of the east is good to warm up on, with fitness growing for the more exciting, tougher, and wetter west. All the guidebooks are eastbound, but the route is on the map, and waymarked on the ground, so that the guidebook description is not crucial.

After a delightful clifftop start at Portpatrick, the Way takes tracks and minor roads round the edge of Stranraer. The first depressing section is over the moors: the placenames along the old leper road are stimulating, but the rough track and trees are not.

The Way enters the Galloway Hills in fine style, with a battlefield traverse above Loch Trool: but then continues on forest road through this most splendid range. A diversion to high Loch Enoch will greatly improve the walk at this point. After St John's Town of Dalry, the route improves. A series of high crossings leads into the Scaur, then the Euchan valley, with a high crossing of the Lowther

APPENDIX A: LONGER OUTINGS

Hills to the Dalveen Pass road. Most of this stretch can be traced on the route maps in sections 4 and 2.

More plantations lead to Beattock, and then up into Ettrick Head. This tight little pass is a brief highlight, but soon gives way to 9 miles of track and road. (Here again, a northern diversion along either Ettrick or Moffat Hills adds considerably to the excitement.)

The Way has now left the area of this guidebook. Grassy high moorlands lead onwards, giving easy and enjoyable walking past St Mary's Loch and by the Minchmoor to Melrose, where the Abbey can be admired from the windows of the youth hostel, and the abrupt Eildon Hills climbed up. Lower hills, field-edges, and the odd pretty wood lead on to the final cliff stretch into Longformacus.

Not the Southern Upland Way

A much better route can be made across the Southern Uplands by keeping, as far as possible, to the higher ground. I have started such a route at Lindisfarne (though Berwick is also a possibility), to take the Border Ridge over the Cheviots and then Cauldcleuch Head. (Alternatively, the Roman Road that is now St Cuthbert's Way leads over Eildon to Melrose, rejoining the SU Way at the start of its best stretch.) The crossing of the Ae Forest is fairly grim, though useful rides do connect the forest roads where required, but the final back-door ascent of Ettrick Pen is a delight.

My preferred route heads out of Beattock onto Queensberry, and uses routes of section 2 to reach Wanlockhead. From Sanquhar, it continues along the crest of the high ground to Carsphairn, and then goes through the heart of the Galloway Hills to Loch Trool. The finest finish is over Cairnsmore of Fleet to reach the sea at Ringdoo Point.

Galloway Coast

I have made occasional attempts to work out a route along the Solway Coast, but the lack of rights-of-way means that some very fine stretches have to be linked with road-walking or muddy struggles along the foreshore.

From the Devorgilla Bridge at Dumfries, the estuary-side path leads downstream to Islesteps. A footpath crosses fields by St Ronan's Well, and lets you into a corner of Mabie Forest (Walk 5:5).

THE LOWTHER HILLS

Walkers are welcome in Shambellie Forest, which leads to New Abbey.

Walk 5:3 now leads up Criffel, and on to Boreland Hill, when a Forest Enterprise trail leads down, mostly on forest road, to Caulkerbrush. Back roads are probably the best way to continue to Sandyhills for the splendid coastal walk (5:7) to Kippford.

Dalbeattie Town Wood is entered at Barnbarroch: its granite craglets and woody pools lead into the town centre.

It's roads or forests - or a mixture - to the foot of Screel (Walk 5:8). From Bengairn, an asserted right-of-way leads down through trees to Hass. Tongland Power Station and the bank of the Dee lead into the very attractive staging-point of Kirkcudbright.

I can recommend no particular route to Gatehouse, but things improve for the crossing of the final, and finest, of the coastal hills. The Corse of Slakes road leads to the base of Cairnsmore of Fleet, which is crossed to Cairnsmore farm (Walks 6:2, 6:1). From Stronord, forest walks lead round Larg Hill, with a path across the golf course to Minnigaff youth hostel.

The "Whithorn Pilgrim Way" runs southwards, but apart from the coastal finale (Walk 6:6) this is almost entirely on roads. So, for the time being, the terminus of my putative Solway Way remains at Newton Stewart.

B: OTHER SPORTS
Skiing

Quite well inland, and with a fair bit of ground over 2000ft (600m), the Lowthers have snow from time to time between January and March.

When there is snow to ski on, the skiing here is rather good. The rounded tops allow uninterrupted day-long journeys: Wanlockhead makes a convenient high start-point. Navigation in mist is a problem for skiers: zigzag descents make it impossible to keep on a compass bearing. Here the Lowthers' fences, and the Harveys map that marks them, are a real aid. Also there's nothing much bigger than a craglet to fall over the top of.

Nordic bindings are appropriate. The abandoned tractor on the slope of Lower Hill was the engine for Wanlockhead's brief but doomed attempt at becoming a downhill ski resort.

APPENDIX B: OTHER SPORTS

Mountain Bike

The Lowther Hills are a superb mountain bike area. Firstly, there are the forest roads; not all of them are submerged in the greenery, and the "Heads of the Valleys" road linking the Kello, Euchan, Scaur and Shinnel is commended to those who like to climb thousands of feet on well-graded gravel track.

Then there are the forest off-roads. There are marked bike trails at Ae, Drumlanrig, Dalbeattie, and Kirroughtree, but devotees of the bloodstained tree-root should head first to Rik's Bike Shed in Mabie Forest, 5 miles (8km) south of Dumfries.

Lovers of rough hill tracks should look at the old roads leading down into Durisdeer. The coach road from the Well Pass has broken two collarbones at least. Good use could also be made of the access track to the Windy Standard turbines.

Hill Running

is the game known as "fellrunning" in England. Races are held on Merrick (Galloway Hills), Criffel, Screel, Tinto and Roan Fell. Details may be obtained from the Scottish Sports Council (South Gyle, Edinburgh) or from the Fell Running Association.

With their long grassy ridges, these hills are particularly suited to non-competitive long runs. A favourite is the complete circuit of the N & S Lowthers, with the SU Way used to link Queensberry and Louise Wood Law. There has been some competition over the four Galloway Corbetts: Cairnsmore of Carsphairn, Corserine, Merrick and Shalloch. The route, from Craigengillan to Stinchar Bridge, also includes Beninner, Cairnsgarroch, Meaul, Carlin's Cairn, Kirriereoch and Tarfessock, and is to be run before the end of February with the snowline at least as low as Loch Enoch. The current record for the 28 miles (45km) and 8000ft (2400m) of climb is 7hrs 42min.

Rock Climbing

Short routes have been recorded at Glenwhargan in the Scaur Valley (not in nesting season, please), at Afton Water, and at Brighouse Bay on the Kirkcudbright coast. More serious (but still rather scrappy) climbs on granite are in the east corrie of Cairnsmore of Fleet.

THE LOWTHER HILLS

Winter Climbing
The only winter climbing (as opposed to winter walking) is on the east face of Cairnsmore of Carsphairn, where steep broken slopes give entertaining cramponing occasionally.

Motoring and Road Cycling
With the sides and bottoms of these hills being, in some respects, their best bits, those who like to experience their hills from behind a windscreen get rather good value. Particularly nice are the single-track road up the Scaur (and cyclists can link this, by the Heads of the Valleys track, with the other single-track road down the Shinnel); the Dalveen and Mennock passes through the Lowthers; and the Hermitage Water road just south of Cauldcleuch Head.

For cyclists, the Solway Coast from Portpatrick to New Abbey is a network of quiet country roads with views of hill and sea. A holiday of a very old-fashioned sort can be enjoyed on bike and hill, linking the youth hostels at Wanlockhead, Kendoon (Dalry) and Minnigaff (Newton Stewart).

Other Sports
Hillwalking can be combined with canoeing (Rivers Nith and Cairn, and coast), dinghy sailing (Loch Ken, Kippford), salmon fishing (Cree, Nith, Annan) and trout fishing (all over the place).

C: TRANSPORT, ACCOMMODATION, INFORMATION
The Nith Valley line (Scotrail) runs through the area, with stations at Dumfries, Sanquhar, Kirkconnel and New Cumnock. Very long cross-country walks could aim for the Ayrshire coastal line. The useful stations are at Barrhill and along the Southern Upland Way at Stranraer.

The area is well served by buses, with daily school buses to many remote points. Intercity coaches link Newton Stewart, Castle Douglas and Dumfries with English cities.

There are youth hostels at Minnigaff (Newton Stewart), Kendoon (Dalry) and Wanlockhead. B&Bs along the SU Way are used to walkers, and the SU Way leaflet is a good starting point for accommodation. The main towns, and the coastal villages, are also accommodating.

APPENDIX C: TRANSPORT, ACCOMMODATION, INFORMATION

Phone Numbers

Rail enquiries	0345 48 49 50
D&G Bus enquiries	0345 090510

Tourist Information
- Dumfries .... 01387 253862 (all year)
- Dumfries brochure request line 0990 134948
- Sanquhar 01659 50185
- Castle Douglas 01556 502611
- Dalbeattie 01556 610117
- Kirkcudbright 01557 330494
- Gatehouse of Fleet 01557 814212
- Langholm 013873 80976

Weather (met office 5-day) 0891 500420

Wind farm opponents: Keep Galloway Beautiful
Barnsoul Farm, Irongray, Dumfries DG2 9SQ

Low flying aircraft queries, complaints:
RAF Community Relations,
Charnwood Rd, Dumfries DG1 3AG 01387 257512

**EMERGENCIES: 999 and ask for
Mountain Rescue (or Coast Rescue)**

IF YOU LIKE ADVENTUROUS ACTIVITIES ON MOUNTAINS OR HILLS YOU WILL ENJOY

Climber

MOUNTAINEERING / HILLWALKING / TREKKING / ROCK CLIMBING / SCRAMBLING IN BRITAIN AND ABROAD

AVAILABLE FROM NEWSAGENTS, OUTDOOR EQUIPMENT SHOPS, OR BY SUBSCRIPTION (6-12 MONTHS) from

**MYATT McFARLANE PLC
PO BOX 28, ALTRINCHAM, CHESHIRE WA14 2FG
Tel: 0161 928 3480   Fax: 0161 941 6897
ISDN No: 0161 926 8937   e-mail: mmpe-mail@aol.com**

THE WALKERS' MAGAZINE

TGO
THE GREAT OUTDOORS

COMPULSIVE MONTHLY READING FOR ANYONE INTERESTED IN WALKING

AVAILABLE FROM NEWSAGENTS, OUTDOOR EQUIPMENT SHOPS, OR BY SUBSCRIPTION (6-12 MONTHS) from

**CALEDONIAN MAGAZINES LTD,
6th FLOOR, 195 ALBION STREET, GLASGOW G1 1QQ
Tel: 0141 302 7700   Fax: 0141 302 7799
ISDN No: 0141 302 7792   e-mail: info@calmags.co.uk**